# THE WEB OF THE UNIVERSE

# THE WEB OF THE UNIVERSE

An Occult Theory of Sub-stance, of Man's Origins and the
Source of his Creative Powers

By

E. L. GARDNER

THE THEOSOPHICAL
PUBLISHING HOUSE, LONDON

68 GREAT RUSSELL STREET
LONDON
W.C.I

*First Published* - - - - - 1936

PRINTED IN GUERNSEY, C.I., BRITISH
ISLES, BY THE STAR AND GAZETTE LTD.

# CONTENTS

# CHARTS, DIAGRAMS AND ILLUSTRATIONS

# ACKNOWLEDGMENTS

My grateful thanks are due to Mr. John Murray for permission to use two illustrations (Nos. 15 and 16) from *Halliburton's Handbook of Physiology*, and to the Christian Herald Co., Ltd., for the two Voice Figure Illustrations (Nos. 14 and 22) from Mrs. Hughes' book, *The Eidophone Voice Figures*.

Also my great indebtedness and sincere thanks to Mr. H. I. Hammond for the special diagrams, Nos. 4, 5, 6, 7, 10, 12, 23, 24 and 25, which elucidate so graphically the relations of the Web and its contents, and to the friends who have generously assisted in the revision of the text.

E.L.G.

# THE WEB OF THE UNIVERSE

# CHAPTER I

## "FATHER-MOTHER SPIN A WEB"

THE *Stanzas of Dzyan,* from which the title of this chapter is taken, are reputed to be the most ancient occult writings in existence. They are described as ". . . an archaic Manuscript—a collection of palm leaves made impermeable to water, fire and air, by some unknown process". Upon them Madame Blavatsky based her book *The Secret Doctrine* and many extracts from them are quoted in both volumes.

Frequently the term—the Web—appears in the Stanzas:

" The Seven were not yet born from the Web of Light. . . .

" Father-Mother spin a Web whose upper end is fastened to Spirit, the Light of the One Darkness, and the lower one to its shadowy end Matter; and this Web is the Universe, spun out of the Two Substances made in One. . . .

" It expands when the Breath of Fire [spirit] is upon it; it contracts when the Breath of the Mother [matter] touches it. . . . When it is cooling it becomes radiant " . . . etc. (From Stanzas II and III.)

It may well be that this Web, with spirit and matter for its warp and woof, is the parent of the Universal Mind, that world of Mind which, following the results of recent scientific research into the nature of physical material, is being so widely inferred to-day.

As above, so below—and the infinitely large may often be found reflected in the infinitely small, as a whole landscape in a dewdrop. The cocoon spun by many of the humblest of creatures as a sacrificial provision for the welfare of their progeny would appear to be itself a minute reflection of that vast and glorious sacrifice made by the Creator, the Father-Mother of our Solar Universe, that a planetary system might be successfully cradled and so become manifest.

The Stanzas proceed to outline a vast scheme of evolutionary processes in which the One becomes Three and then Seven; the sequences which follow are also based on recurrent septenary systems.

The states of consciousness possible to man and the primary modifications of natural forces, as well as the worlds of the Solar System with which we are concerned, are each said to be seven in number. Similarly, septenates are said to mark every branch of manifestation—all are sequences of seven factors. The seven colours of the light spectrum and the octaves of music are among the many correspondences which may be taken as familiar examples.

Accepting the monistic theory of One Life, let us attempt the contemplation of One becoming Seven. This, if we grant the possibility of motion and therefore the possibility of manifestation within the One, is comparatively easy. Let a pencil point touching a paper surface represent One. Move the point and a line appears. At once the number three is in evidence, the two termini of the line, themselves two points, and the line itself. Two extremes are there and the relating line between them. As the principal permutations of three factors are numerically seven, the septenate system of manifestation seems at least reasonable. Assuming three factors —for example, A, B and C, to be equal in value—they can be arranged in order of dominance as ABC, ACB, BAC, BCA, CAB, CBA, six in all; to these add their synthesis with " no one before the other " and we have the seventh. The formula is $1 \times 2 \times 3 + 1 = 7$. Within the seven, relationships may be noted of 3 to 4 and of 2 to 5, both of significance.

Another illustration will assist here. Man, as a constructional creator, uses his hands. Though his creations are extended indefinitely by means of tools and machines, all he makes derives from the hands; they are the original creative instruments. Now the whole arm is divisible into three parts —the upper arm, the lower arm and the hand. We have therefore in this example a main group of three—and the third member of this trinity, the hand, is divided further into five, the fingers. This last group of five is the immediately active creative agent. Such an analogy, or correspondence, affords some assistance to an understanding of the Three-in-One relationship of the original creative principle. The upper arm, for instance, is the seat of power for its septenary group; the lower arm is adaptable and flexible, is anatomically dual, and is capable of skilful direction; the five-fingered hand is the actively creative medium. Here is a close resemblance to the description of the One becoming Seven.

From a study of the occult instructions the inference is irresistible that in the arm and hand of man, viewed as his means for the creation of forms at the physical level, we have a true correspondence, as far as it goes, with the plan of Creative Manifestation. Of the seven planes and principles of a Solar System, two are said to be hidden, " in Silence and Darkness " are the terms used with reference to them; five are actively manifest. Hence the statement, so common in certain eastern philosophies, that we live at present in a five-fold universe.

In our example, if we assume for a moment the point of view of one of man's creations, say a piece of sculpture, then to it the upper and lower arm would be " beyond ", out of view, for the five-fingered hand would appear to be the immediate and only creative cause of its existence. Similarly, to us, within and about us is evidence of a five-fold creative activity. We are conscious (not necessarily self-conscious) in five different states of consciousness or planes, namely, physical, emotional, mental, intuitional and volitional; the corresponding five occult centres in man are more or less active and we have five senses or avenues of contact with the physical world.

Two planes and two principles, the Divine and Monadic, (Adi-Anupadaka) are at present beyond, unknown, " in silence ". But a vast work of theirs, indeed that which makes the very field of our five-fold manifestation possible, would seem to be the Web spun by them within which and by means of which, as a scriptural phrase has it, we live and move and have our being. They are the two subtler and most deeply occult principles of our Solar Universe and are symbolised by Father-Mother in the Stanzas quoted. They support the whole as the arm carries the hand. A description of the pattern and the function of their Web is attempted in this book.

# CHAPTER II

## SOME DESCRIPTIVE DEFINITIONS

IN the later *Stanzas of Dzyan* there is a description, heavily veiled in symbolism, of the process by which forms come into manifestation and of the elaborate seven-fold scheme of evolution in which our human consciousness is taking its assigned part.

In an appendix to this book a summary is given of the vast cycles of manifestation known as Chains and Rounds in modern occult writings. The summary is necessarily in very general terms, but a perusal will enable the reader to grasp in broad outline the nature of some of the closely guarded secrets imparted in olden times to the initiates of various Mystery Schools under stringent vows of silence. The veil of secrecy has been lifted from time to time, as minor cycles have run their course, and we are to-day at liberty to examine and analyse and, so far as may be possible, to test some of the instructions given. Although these are said to be the result of experienced investigation the student is invariably advised to receive the information as hypothetical and theoretical only, till enabled by his own researches to accept or reject. Till then a suspended judgment is the wisest course. This interpretation of the Web of the Universe is submitted in all sincerity but with the same reservation.

In order to avoid misunderstandings this chapter is devoted to giving a few descriptive definitions of some more or less familiar terms that are used in this book and are met with frequently in occult literature. A chart also is given (No. I) which displays the seven-fold and the five-fold relationships of the Worlds and the Principles of Man.*

* The reading and study of this chapter and of the appendix may be postponed if preferred. They are both explanatory of terms used and reference can be made to them as required. They are not essential, though useful, to the general exposition.

13

# THE WEB OF THE UNIVERSE

## CHART OF THE WORLDS OR PLANES AND THE HUMAN PRINCIPLES AND BODIES CORRESPONDING

### OUR SOLAR SCHEME : SEVEN-FOLD SYSTEM

|  | Eastern Terms | English Terms |
|---|---|---|
| The Monad's Birth-Place | ADI | DIVINE |
|  | ANUPADAKA | MONADIC |
|  | ATMA | SPIRITUAL |
|  | BUDDHI | INTUITIONAL |
|  | MANAS | MENTAL |
|  | KAMA | EMOTIONAL (ASTRAL) |
|  | SHARIRA | PHYSICAL |

---

### THE FOURTH CHAIN OF THE SOLAR SCHEME : OUR TERRENE CHAIN.  A FIVE-FOLD SYSTEM

| | | | |
|---|---|---|---|
| 1. The | Ego | ATMA | SPIRITUAL |
| 2. Higher | | BUDDHI | INTUITIONAL |
| 3. Self | | MANAS I | HIGHER MENTAL |
| 3. The | Personality | MANAS II | LOWER MENTAL |
| 4. Lower | | KAMA | EMOTIONAL (ASTRAL) |
| 5. Self | | LINGA SHARIRA | ETHERIC PHYSICAL |
| Synthesis in Form | | STHULA SHARIRA | DENSE PHYSICAL |

---

We are said to be in the Fourth or Middle Round of our Terrene Chain: hence, during our present occupation of our planet Earth, we are functioning at the densest levels of our whole Scheme.  As four planes only are normally used in the same Round Cycle it follows that, during this world-occupation, humanity is consciously engaged actively on the levels of the Lower Mental, the Astral and the two divisions of the Physical.  Beginning now, however, to climb in consciousness the upward arc of the cycle, the Higher Mental is the spiritual principle ahead as the next goal to reach.  Thus the following gives the current and immediate relationships—

Higher Self        Ego    HIGHER MENTAL (Buddhi-Manas)

Lower Self        Personality    LOWER MENTAL BODY
EMOTIONAL (ASTRAL) BODY
ETHERIC PHYSICAL BODY

Synthetic Vehicle, DENSE PHYSICAL BODY

Number One

14

# SOME DESCRIPTIVE DEFINITIONS

## LIFE

Spirit undifferentiated. The One Life. God.

## CONSCIOUSNESS

A ray of the One Life separated from the ocean of life by association and identification with Forms. Hence awareness, a vague and diffused consciousness, is awakened. Examples: The Mineral, Plant and Animal Kingdoms on an increasingly conscious scale.

## SELF-CONSCIOUSNESS

The very definite and clear-cut association of Life or Spirit with a form-body, a personality, is the means by which consciousness distinguishes between itself in its own separate abode or body and all other bodies—and thus is individualised and becomes *self*-conscious. Example: Humanity.

## THE POSITION OF OUR EARTH

Four of the seven Chains of our Scheme are shown diagrammatically on Chart No. 2. This is to illustrate the statement that the seven globes of Chain IV are manifest in four planes only and these the densest of our Scheme.

In the first Chain of our Solar Scheme, its one and only globe was of mental material. The whole vast period of that first Chain's work, *in terms of form*, was the creation of a single planet and its modest contents. The second Chain had three globes of form and the third had five. Being now on the fourth Chain of the Scheme we profit greatly from the work of our predecessors on the first three Chains and have seven planets of material form to use, built of the material of four planes. Chart No. 2 displays this in a diagram that Mr. A. P. Sinnett* always insisted was the only correct way to chart the successive Chains of Globes.

---

* *Esoteric Buddhism*, by A. P. Sinnett, was one of the very first Theosophical publications in the west.

## OUR TERRENE SCHEME

| CHAIN I | II | III | IV | |
|---|---|---|---|---|
| Mental | o | o  o | o  o | o  o  Chains V, VI, VII |
| | | | | in future |
| Astral | | o | o  o | o  o |
| | | | | |
| Phys. I | | . | o | o  o |
| | | | | |
| Phys. II | | | | o – – –>  Our earth. |

One    Three   Five    Seven
Globe  Globes  Globes  Globes

Number Two

Whether these material globes, in their inter-relations within each Chain, be regarded as concentric (Steiner) or spatially separate (Sinnett and Leadbeater), does not here concern us: the important feature is that the first world to be built and hence the first and earliest plane of form is stated to be mental. It may therefore reasonably be inferred that all material globes of form arise from modifications of what Mme. Blavatsky called Lower Manas (The Lower Mind or Mental II.). This is the subtlest of the worlds of form.

FORMS AND THE FORMLESS

As the successive Chains of globes are described as being always concerned with four planes it is obvious, from Diagram No. 2, that the work of the First Chain, though possessing but one globe of form, is also on three planes above the lower mental. But all above the lower mental is held to be of a " formless " nature. Let us therefore attempt to dispose of the difficulty which may very naturally arise from the use of the word " formless ".

This word has been frequently used to distinguish the inner or subtler spiritual planes, that is, the divine life unmanifested to normal vision, from that of material form—and a rather puzzling conception is thereby offered to the student. Formlessness implies no thing, no separated feature of manifestation whatever, yet several of such planes are named and these presumably differ! The explanation is however not far to seek and we need to be at the outset entirely clear as to the reason for the use of this somewhat misleading descriptive term. An analogy will most easily clarify the position. Consider the relation of a pencil point to paper as an illustration of the connection between the higher and the lower mental planes. The pencil point can very reasonably be called formless: but it is capable of creating form on paper. Move the pencil point and under a skilled hand an elaborate form design emerges. If it be conceived as moving with extreme rapidity we should witness what would approximate to an instantaneous drawing, and apparently *ex nihilo*! Endow the pencil point in imagination with the speed of light and we should approach a comparison with the inter-action of the higher and lower mental principles—for the higher mental centre apparently can move at that prodigious speed.

Man, being a reflection of the universe in miniature, also has his formless spiritual nature, and the bodies of form which it uses make up his personality. From the point of view of this personality (for we are at present largely confined to these slow and ponderous personal bodies of physical, emotional and mental material), we can best picture higher mental activity as due to a brilliant point of light. This expresses the human spiritual self, the spark of the divine flame; this is the true centre of consciousness of a human being however much, in ignorance of his true nature, he may be identified with bodies of form. The human spirit is formless in itself, as is the pencil point, but capable readily of creating form on the screen of the lower mind—and a form, too, of three dimensions that has a considerable " lag " of persistence, like the lag of an impression on the retina of the eye.

Many a similar analogy could be employed—such as the light from a cinema lantern and the screen on which the picture is thrown. The light is formless until it is arrested and held. Both light and screen are needed for the creation of a flowing picture. The two together provide the mechanism for the manifestation of forms. The light symbolises the higher, the screen represents the lower mind. It is by the study of such analogies that the term " formless " becomes understandable.

## THE ELEMENTS AND TATTVAS

Authorities in occultism describe the three worlds of form, physical, emotional and mental, as distinguishable by their specific " measure " or " tattva ". This refers to the mode of motion, the rhythmic movement, the measure, of their material composition, for the units of each are said to have a dominant and characteristic *tattva*. The ancient occult teaching that material is really motion or energy, though commonplace to-day, is less than fifty years old in our western science. These measures or tattvas have their minor correspondences again on each plane, and those with which we are most familiar are the sub-states of physical material which we call solid, liquid and gaseous. Concerning the larger divisions of our three-fold world the solid (prithivi) tattva is dominantly characteristic of the physical, the liquid (apas) tattva of the astral, and the gaseous (tejas) tattva of the mental. Another series in correspondence are the so-called elements of nature—earth, water, fire and air. Each has a significant sign or symbol—a square, a crescent, a triangle. The following chart displays these correspondences :

| Plane | PHYSICAL | EMOTIONAL | MENTAL |
|---|---|---|---|
| Element | EARTH | WATER | FIRE |
| Tattva | PRITHIVI | APAS | TEJAS |
| Phys. sub-state | SOLID | LIQUID | GASEOUS |
| Symbol of Tattva | SQUARE | HALF-CIRCLE | TRIANGLE |
| Geometrical Figure | CUBE | ICOSAHEDRON | OCTAHEDRON |

NOTE : With reference to the element " air ", at present fire and air are almost interchangeable terms. Cold flame is an occult term for air on certain occasions, on others air (vayu tattva) is classified as a higher element than fire. In our own present cycle, the deepest in material form, air is fire grown cold, hence the correspondence of true fire with the " mental " in this chart.

# SOME DESCRIPTIVE DEFINITIONS

In *The Secret Doctrine*, Vol. I, 273, H.P.B. states that the "correct order for esoteric purposes is fire, air, water, earth." Esoteric purposes means the order in which, in the beginning of our cycle, they manifested. Fire first—and the tejas tattva, its measure of motion, has a triangle for its symbol. The triangle in this connection may be taken as the flat figure representative of the octahedron, the occult geometrical "unit" of the mental world. The appropriateness of this octahedral correspondence with the mind will emerge in our study.

## Our Three-fold Planet

That our familiar material world is not only physical but has a mental and emotional content too, also of material, may quite well be inferred from the fact that man has a mental and emotional nature in addition to a physical body. But thought and feeling have been so related to and indeed identified with the brain and nervous systems that the inference is by no means universally made.

A difficulty which prevents a general acceptance of this view is doubtless the concept of a *material* mind—yet recorded experiences of consciousness, apart from the physical brain and body and quite independent of both, are many and increasingly frequent.

The concept of our world as three-fold means that in combination with the physical earth there are also worlds (or planes) interacting with it of mental and emotional material. This is a logical assumption to-day in the light of our modern knowledge concerning material itself, for, resolved into energy as it is, the long standing materialistic concept of the universe disappears.

Energy, Motion, Life, call it what we will, alone remains—and a fuller understanding of many a mental and emotional problem would follow if the concept of energy was extended to include extremely subtle varieties of material whose tattvas or measures of vibratory response were emotional and mental in quality. As differences in the elements of physical material are now known to be due to differences in wave motions or energy, an extension of the same concept provides us with the distinction between one interpenetrating world of experience and another, which is relatively easy to comprehend.

In this connection a very appropriate analogy and example is afforded by the Radio System and a wireless receiving set. When an efficient set is tuned in to a particular programme every other is ignored. Though capable of reproducing many programmes, all of which are being broadcasted at the same time, one alone comes through. This obviously depends entirely on the degree of selectivity of the machine.

Very similarly, on the large scale of the planes of nature, though we live in three material worlds at once we are conscious with clarity and precision of one only, the physical. We are at present, fortunately, unable easily to tune into the other two. Control and mastery of mind and emotion, that is, selective skill in listening in to these worlds of experience, are essential to avoid confusion and its possible consequence—insanity. Hence though the mental and emotional planes are interwoven intimately with the physical they are very naturally translated and interpreted in the terms of our familiar physical senses and physical brain consciousness. Of the three worlds separated from each other by differences of wave motion only, as an examination of the Web will explain, two are not clearly apprehended and known by themselves as yet. We function in them directly after what we call " death ", and the intermediate periods between physical incarnations have special value for this reason. While in physical bodies however this selective skill and distinction still awaits the development of other faculties—probably the sixth and seventh senses.

## PERSONALITY

This term is used in the literal sense of *per sona*, the mask behind or within which the real man acts. The personality technically consists of the abodes or bodies in which a man

20

normally lives and includes therefore the physical, emotional and mental bodies of a human being functioning on corresponding planes. These three planes or worlds in combination, as has just been said, constitute our material earth planet.

### HIGHER AND LOWER SELF (See Chart on page 14)

These terms are convenient and perhaps permissible as distinguishing the spiritual principles of man from the personal. But they are unfortunate in the implied disparagement of the so-called "lower". The spiritual principles of man, the spiritual, intuitional and higher mental, derived from the One Life, owe whatever self-realisation they attain to their formal projection into the bodies that we call the personality (the lower self). This latter is the mirror in which alone spirit can see, apprehend and hence *know* itself. To view the personality as "lower" in the sense of inferior is as though we exalted the lantern of a cinema theatre and disparaged the screen which alone enables the picture to be seen at all. Both the spiritual focus of light, the Ego, and the Personality that reflects the focused light are equally necessary to the Source of Light, the One Life. Hence we should not allow the terms higher and lower to connote superiority and inferiority. With this reservation the terms may be accepted as conventionally useful.

### SUBJECTIVE AND OBJECTIVE

Subjective experiences are those which are interior, or seemingly interior, to oneself, that is, are within one's own consciousness, such as experiences of thinking and feeling. Though every experience may be claimed to be subjective in essence, as indeed is obviously the case, it is usual to define as objective that part of the environment which is recognised in experience as *being* environment. This is to say that, from a state of complete subjectivity in which we began, humanity has succeeded in relating clearly a certain group of inner experiences to an external world, namely, the physical.

Hence the physical world is commonly held to be objective. Further, with many, the physical body itself is becoming objective—as consciousness, by withdrawal, succeeds in externalising its reactions. With still further success on these lines, though it will be much later for most of us, the emotional and mental worlds will become objective and known as environment.

Objectivity of the emotional and mental worlds is now called psychism, or psychic faculty, and is often accidental and embarrassing to the individual if this inner sight has been opened prematurely without adequate control and understanding of the situation. In due course the race will be normally and rationally psychic, which means that, in their turn, man's own emotional and mental bodies will be known as not being the real Self. Thus the process upon which humanity is at present engaged is apparently an ordered withdrawal—as the objective environment increases and the subjective field diminishes.

Consciousness is amply compensated for this seeming transfer from subjective to objective by its increasing sensitiveness and speed of response to contacts made. Put in another way, consciousness withdraws from a periphery, to which it has been " tempted " by the bodies it uses, to a centre, whence it emerged from Life as a point of living light, and brings with it on its return the jewel of great price, the faculty of responding to the whole content of the objective worlds at will.

That point of living light, a unit of subjective consciousness, by identifying itself with bodies succeeds in " becoming a sphere ". Then, on the return journey, it proceeds to externalise the sphere, beginning with the outermost layers, and thus breaks down the great illusion of its identification with matter. The point thus first becomes the sphere and then re-becomes the point.

By thus realising the material worlds of the physical, the emotional and the mental as being objective to itself, the eternal spark regains the tremendous facilities of a point of life with the whole content of the sphere at its service. That attainment ultimately spells omnipresence—the first of the divine faculties to be unfolded in man.

### PERMANENT ATOMS AND SKANDHAS

Permanent atom is the technical term applied to that atom or unit of each of the personal planes (mental, astral or physical) which is retained life after life for the use of the reincarnating spirit or ego—and which contains within itself the record of all past experience. It therefore provides the plan on which the new body for the use of the egoic consciousness on each plane may be accurately built for the next incarnation.

For many students the difficulty of this theory has been the retention of the permanent atom by consciousness while functioning on higher planes. Where, for instance, is the physical permanent atom when one is in devachan? How can an atom of a material plane be held there?

The difficulty is however more apparent than real, though in some quarters it has led to a rejection of the whole theory of the permanent atom as an adequate explanation of continuity in human evolution. But one would be equally justified in rejecting the equator or the north pole on the score that neither has ever been exhibited in support of an explorer's claim. The answer is of course that these terms all indicate a locus, a position, a focus of power, not a *thing*.

In illustration, place an ordinary bar magnet underneath a paper covered with iron filings—and the fragments of iron will at once display themselves in a formal pattern. They obey the forces playing within the magnet's sphere of influence. Move the magnet about and all the iron filings within the field of the magnet respond. The iron fragments change but the regular form-pattern continues the same. The magnetic forces of the bar determine the response. Similarly the magnetic field of the human point of life compels a corresponding response at the atomic level of the plane. To change the simile—the skill of an artist in painting does not reside in his paint and implements, he does not need to carry a " permanent " pencil or crayon about with him, the colour and tools he uses respond to the living magnetic field of his creative ability. The human aura in devachan displays the permanent atom in terms of lines of force—just as the active field of a magnet may be seen by a clairvoyant without any material filings.

Skandhas are those deeply impressed formations, in any plane, made by human consciousness and held more or less intact by the elemental life of the same plane over the interval between lives. They tend to attach themselves again to their human creator when next he appears at the same level, as they naturally are in tune with him—and possibly with him alone. The skandha is thus an artificial form held intact for a more or less lengthy period and may function as a mere tendency and influence or act as a veritable " dweller on the threshold ".

The permanent atom and the skandhas are the formal responses to the behaviour of consciousness; lack of skill is represented by deficiences and possibly a tendency to distortion. While being a useful convention as a term, the permanent atom really represents a formal pattern imposed by the electric, magnetic or vital forces which constitute the active field, the aura, of a human being when using the personal planes.

## THE PLATONIC SOLIDS AND THE OCCULT CROSS

Our sense impressions are normally so direct, precise and familiar that we take very much for granted that things are what they seem—until maybe an analysis is prompted by some startling statement we read or hear concerning the illusions to which our senses are subject. Then perhaps for a while we ponder on the shadowy nature of material things and, if introspective, on the unreality of the world we live in. Matter is said to be very different from that which we believed it to be : our physical senses have deceived us thoroughly in this : material is really energy exhibiting itself, simply energy —and mental at that !

In recent years the reduction of material things into terms of the mind has been the theme not only of philosophers, religiously minded and otherwise, but of the practical and exacting scientist.

" The universe shows evidence of a designing or controlling power that has something in common with our own individual minds." " The universe can be best pictured as consisting of pure thought." " If the universe is a universe of thought then its creation must have been an act of thought."

wrote Sir James Jeans in 1934 in *The Mysterious Universe* (pp. 124-137). And Sir J. A. Thompson concluded a contribution to *The Great Design*, published in 1934, with these words : " we are led from our own mind back and back to the Supreme mind, ' without whom there was nothing made that was made '." Similar reflections are to be found in many current scientific articles.

It is therefore an opportune moment to consider the relevant information at hand from metaphysical and occult sources and to point to the conclusions which may fairly be drawn.

First we must touch on the well-known regular figures of geometry known as the Platonic Solids, five in number, which have in each case equal facets, equal angles and equal lines. These five regular solids are here illustrated (No. 3).

The tetrahedron, or four-sided figure, with which the series begins is also their basic form, as the four others may all be constructed on combinations of the tetrad as shown in the illustration.

Size is of no consequence; minute or huge the characteristics apply. It is therefore the interior structure that counts and this is based on a centre whence lines ray out equally

25

spaced. Such a figure is shown in No. 4, with six lines springing from the centre and touching the points of an octahedron, the interior structure thereby forming a solid cross. About the same cross a cube also can be built, because the octahedron and the cube are complementary figures. The cube has six sides and eight points whereas the octahedron has eight sides and six points.

In occult science these regular figures are held to be symbols of the Five Planes of Nature, thus:

Tetrahedron—Atma: Dodecahedron—Buddhi: Octahedron—Mental: Icosahedron—Astral: Hexahedron (Cube) —Physical.

The implication is that the shape of the figure is related intimately to the mode of motion, the tattva, that differentiates one plane from another. In the definition given of the tattva it will be remembered that the distinction between the planes is one of motion, of specific vibratory measure called a tattva, the planes differing radically in this respect. The regular figures symbolise this distinction. In the tetrahedron a flat equal-armed cross is suggested by its lines. Place, for example, two match sticks across each other at right angles in the middle, then raise one a short distance and in imagination connect the four extremities of the matches—a tetrad is formed. Note, for example, the tetrad illustrated on the second line of the illustration opposite. Two tetrahedra, interlaced together as also shown, give the regular figure of the cube if the eight points of the two interlocked tetrads be joined. They indicate the octahedron too if the eight points are taken as the middle of eight equilateral triangles, for the triangles will precisely fit together and an eight-sided regular figure will be duly formed.

Further, inasmuch as both the icosahedron and dodecahedron are built up on five interlaced tetrads (as shown on the third line of the illustration), it is clear that *all* the regular figures owe their formation to simple or compound crosses.

THE FIVE
PLATONIC
SOLIDS

In each solid, lines, angles and surfaces are equal.

Fig.1 Tetrahedron. Fig.2 Cube. Fig.3 Octahedron. Fig.4 Dodecahedron. Fig.5 Icosahedron.

Tetrahedron.

2 Tetrahedra interlaced.

5 Tetrahedra interlaced.

Cube.

Octahedron.

Dodecahedron.

Icosahedron.

Fig. 1—4 Surfaces
Fig. 2— 6 Surfaces
Fig. 3— 8 Surfaces
Fig. 4—12 Surfaces
Fig. 5—20 Surfaces

In other words, in terms of form, all the regular figures owe their origin to a cruciform base.

The widespread symbolism of the cross, far ante-dating the Christian era, has been consistently used to typify the descent of life into matter or form—and thus life's crucifixion or imprisonment. The adoption and use of the cross-symbol is well justified, for its origin may be traced, as we shall see, to the Web woven by Father-Mother, the planetary web that is itself at the very root of material and hence of form.

Of the regular figures it is the octahedron that is of immediate interest in our study.

Number Four

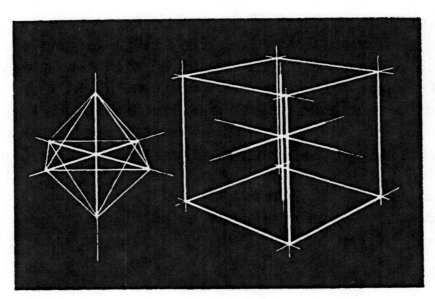

The six-armed cross inside, with arms of equal length at right angles to each other, exactly fits each of these solid figures. In the Octad the six arms touch the points and in the Cube the six arms touch the middle of the facets. The two crosses are of the same size.

The appropriateness of the eight-sided regular figure, the octahedron, as representing the mental principle appeals at once by virtue of its double-pyramid appearance. No figure could more aptly indicate the dual character of mind—the higher and lower—a duality, yet a unity. We need to examine this regular figure closely.

The Octahedron has eight faces, each an equilateral triangle, and six points. The six points represent the extremities of a three-dimensional cross formed by three intersecting lines at right angles to each other. We have therefore in the interior supporting structure of the octad, at the heart of and indeed the cause of its being, three lines of extension which correspond with what are popularly known as the three dimensions of space. A central junction-point is common to the three lines and this point well symbolises the connecting link or portal between a world of form, represented by the regular figures, and the higher and formless planes of life. In the diagram No. 10 this point corresponds to the junction portal between Mental I and II. In the division of the mental plane into higher and lower, three sub-planes are allocated to the higher and four to the lower. We will number them from the atomic or finest downwards, 1, 2, 3, and 4, 5, 6, 7. Those called the 4th, 5th, 6th and 7th sub-planes in this classification constitute the field of the Lower Mind—H.P.B.'s Lower Manas. The intimate relation of these four sub-planes respectively with the junction-point and the three intersecting right-angular lines is very appropriate,

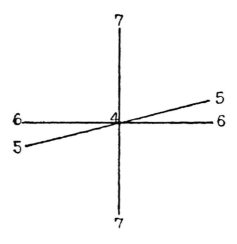

especially as the junction-point—the bridge or link between higher and lower—answers exactly to the characteristics of every " 4th ", for the fourth factor of any septenary series exercises the function of a bridge. It links together two opposites, in this case the higher and lower mental planes. Such a link or bridge is a very important factor in septenary systems.


Let us now attempt to visualise the truly amazing web or fabric supporting the mental, the astral and the physical planes, the substance for all the forms of the three worlds, the canvas on and within which, as in a mirror, life projects its own picture.

CHAPTER III

## THE WEB

THE basic pattern of the Web is the six-armed Cross of the octahedron, infinitely repeated, and appears as a maze of exceedingly fine lines, interlaced in an infinitesimal rectangular texture, ablaze with tiny points of brilliance where the lines cross, filling, enveloping all space and serving as the foundational structure for all material—a vision of mystery and wonder.

> "Father-Mother spin a Web . . . this Web is the Universe . . . it expands with Fire . . . it contracts . . . Fohat traces spiral lines . . . Thought is the rider . . . an Army of the Sons of Light stands at each angle . . . said the Flame to the Spark thou art my image, I have clothed myself in thee . . . it journeys through the worlds . . . stops in the First and is a Metal, a Stone . . . it passes into the Second and behold a Plant . . . the Plant becomes a Sacred Animal . . . from the combined attributes of these Man the Thinker is formed. . . ." *Stanzas Dzyan III-VII.*

It may be reasonably inferred that the Father-Mother (of the *Stanzas of Dzyan*) are no other than Adi-Anupadaka (See No. 1), the two highest principles of our Solar Scheme, and that the Web actually represents, *is* indeed their personal aspect or Lower Self. Such visions of the immediacy and intimacy of the Divine Spirit as in Tennyson's " Closer is He than breathing and nearer than hands and feet ", would seem to derive their inspiration from this omnipresent offspring of Solar parents.

This Web would seem to be the major of " the enormous mysteries connected with Lower Manas " to which H.P.B. referred (*S.D. III*, 592), for it provides the background, the basic foundation for all manifestation as we know it. The junction-points of the three-dimensional crosses very aptly represent the middle of the mental plane, the junction of higher and lower manas, the threshold of the form-worlds, for they are the very portals of approach between spirit and matter. The One Life becomes Many in terms of form as it alights at these portals of the Web to begin its far-reaching excursion into the realm of separated form experiences. The mechanism of the Web permits and invites an immensely elaborate oratorio of manifestation—yet itself throughout remaining unaffected, unaffected as the strings of a harp may be regarded as undisturbed by the melody arising from them. Rigid too as the strings of a well-tuned musical instrument yet with an infinitely varied capacity of vibration.

An examination of the Web reveals that this vast fabric woven by the Father-Mother of our system is relatively fixed, static, immovable. It is a unity which we all share, as railway trains share a permanent way and motor-cars the roads. Forms, whether of thought pulses, astral waves, or physical spirals, all play through the Web as waves do through water, wind through grass or corn, as the circling lights of a Piccadilly advertisement. The water, the grass and corn, the light-bulbs of the advertisement, not one of these moves forward though they all appear so to do. And the forms which use the Web are similar. All are modifications of the Web, all use this responsive net-work, and all are, in a certain and obvious sense, illusory. Thought seems to have the characteristics of electric pulses through a wire, the emotions are wavelike and undulatory, and physical matter shapes itself in rings and spirals, in unclosed spheres something like a thread of cotton wound round a pencil. Hold a length of cotton at both ends tightly, take a round pencil and turn the thread once or twice round it and then move the pencil to and fro, and the spiral of thread moves retaining accurately its shape though flowing along the cotton. Such illustrations and

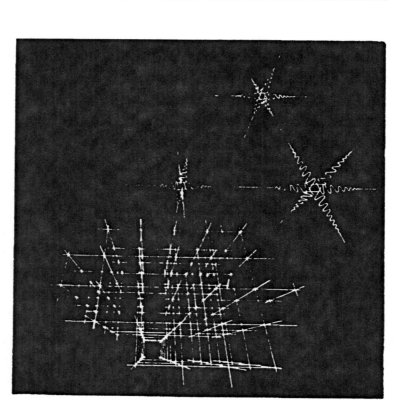

Number Five

Number Six

A PERSPECTIVE VIEW OF THE WEB. THE ENLARGED
CROSSES SHOW THE WAVES OF THE ASTRAL TATTVA

PORTIONS OF THE WEB IN LARGER DETAIL

experiments assist one to build an intellectual conception of the Web—though nothing within the range of our slow-moving sense apparatus can convey the exquisite perfection and delicacy of this skeleton framework, the stage on which the living forms of consciousness dance in the ballet of life.

It must be clearly understood that the Web is sub-stance: it is not itself that which we know as material but *stands under* material. That which we call material is motion of or within the Web in three characteristic modes. The Web itself is the necessary and amazingly adequate background; it corresponds in purpose to the canvas of the painter, the clay of the sculptor, language for the poet, the orchestra for the musician, to the screen at the cinema, the carrier wave for broadcasting. All these are the sub-stance that is necessary for art to manifest, that enables creation to be, to exist, to stand forth. On the larger scale the Web corresponds to the Aether of Space, to Mulaprakriti, to the Feminine Aspect. In relation to the physical, astral and mental planes, the Web is as the very Root of Matter.

The three modes of motion in the Web, the three tattvas, offer a fascinating field of study. Thought, as initiated by humanity when the higher-mind plays on the Web, moves in straight lines and tends to reproduce itself on touching another mental body—much as the lines of light from a lantern slide reproduce the picture on reaching the screen. Whether the reproduction is " received " by another's mind depends entirely on development and acquired skill. In our present cycle the reproduction by the large majority is usually ignored because of preoccupation, or is received merely as a quite unconsciously registered influence.

The basic physical units (the occultist's ultimate physical atoms), which in their aggregate make up what we call physical matter, are produced by atmic force operating in spirals. The wires of the Web do not move but the power current pursues apparently a curved course, leaping spirally from junction-point to junction-point, dividing into three in between,

33

passing along three connecting lines, to join up again at the diagonally opposite corners of the cube.

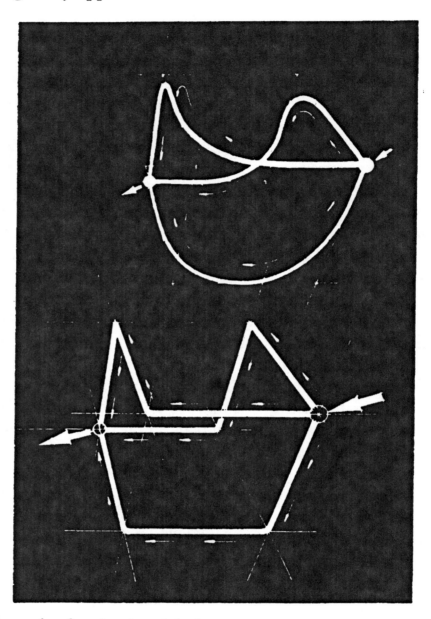

Number Seven

The path taken by the triple force current is shown in the figures above. The arrows indicate the three directions taken, which may be described thus—

One Third (say Red) travels Width Height Depth
One Third (say Yeo) travels Height Depth Width
One Third (say Blue) travels Depth Width Height

It will be noted that each colour is at right angles to the other two all the way and each traverses the three dimensions. Further, if a large number of models, in wire, similar to the above left-hand figure, are assembled together, then it will be found that a triple line, of the three colours, is traced in all directions. At the cross over points only do the colours unite and the dominance of one causes the spiral bias.

The flashes of light when the junction-points are touched by the triple current alone mark the path taken, and these appear like streaming beads of light in lines spirally curved. Three lines or pulses of this atmic force play side by side and occasion in some way, possibly by induction, an additional group roughly parallel with themselves—hence is produced

Number Eight

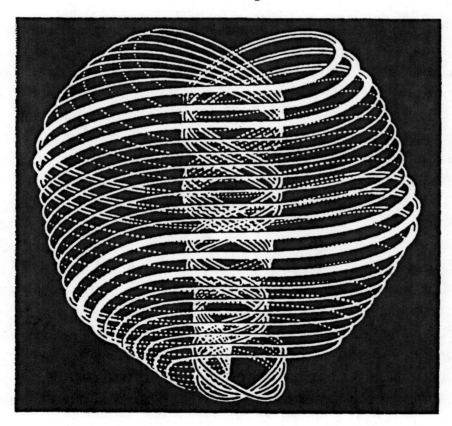

A CLAIRVOYANT'S VISION OF AN ULTIMATE PHYSICAL ATOM

the physical atom itself, a complicated group of swiftly turning wavelets through the Web.

The apas tattva, the astral, is quite different. This alone appears to be an actual vibratory movement of the lines—as shown in Nos. 5 and 6. Buddhi-Astral are the life side of the egoic and personal principles respectively and profoundly affect the content of the Web. The impetus given at one junction appears to be transmitted through the elastic framework as a sound-wave is transmitted from one molecule to another in air or steel. Such waves are those of emotion, which are longitudinal in the framework of the Web. Electrical pulses of thought and the spiral units displaying physical inertia are, so to speak, the boundaries or extremes of the activity in the Web. Buddhi-Astral impulses constitute the life side and are the important content of the Web, though very dominantly *astral* in this cycle. Humanity, as the bridge between the spiritual and the personal, has to forge the union of these two principles, Buddhi-Astral, in himself—and this he must achieve through thought and action, through the mind and the physical body, on the stage of the Web.

The lines of which this intricate mechanism is composed are seemingly rigid, taut-strung, yet exquisitely delicate and fragile. The fragility is an illusion, however, due to the superlative sensitiveness of the glowing lines—lines which are not as a continuous thread but are the effect produced by pulses of force of inconceivable number and rapidity. The lines are spaced regularly apart, though the spacing must be far smaller than even the atomic order of measurement.*

The Web appears to be relatively perfect in construction— perfect that is in the sense that a craftsman's tools may be perfectly suited to his craft. The trained and the untrained workman though using exactly the same tools produce very different results. The quality of the work turned out obviously depends on the craftsman's skill. The same is it with any

* Divide a length of one inch into five hundred million parts, then one part is the estimated radius of a hydrogen atom, the physicist's basis of atomic measurement.

musical instrument, say a finely built organ : the result when used turns on the skill of the musician; the organ is the same for beginner and expert. Applying these analogies to the Web and our very amateur use of its wonderful content, the situation becomes clear, especially as we may well regard the Web as an exquisitely tuned and responsive musical instrument. It is we who make the disharmonies, the strains and distortions; these are no more inherent in this sub-stance of the worlds than faulty discords in the instruments of an orchestra.

Such is a theory of the structure and nature of the underlying field, the basic canvas for the pictures of form. It is this that furnishes the sub-stance on which everything in the three worlds of the mental, astral and physical is built. For the material of these worlds consists purely and wholly of movements within the Web—pulses, waves and spirals—which play freely and easily over and through the Web, governed and limited only by the laws of its construction and the skill of consciousness.

The illustration reproduced overleaf has an interesting bearing on our subject for it illustrates the extensive research work being devoted to the structure of physical material.

The figures are taken from the Chemical Society *Transactions*, by Sir William Bragg. They show the theoretical structure of crystalline forms. Such forms are said to be based on what are called space-lattice patterns. It is significant that a modern theory of spatially extended physical units should demand a backing, a ground-plan as it were, of the cubic and regular spaced character described as being that of the Web.

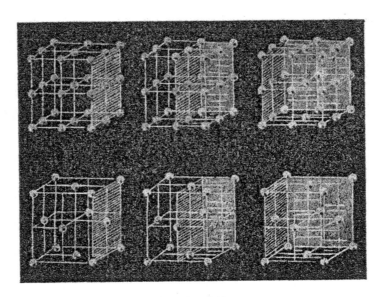

Number Nine

A propos of this and the possibility of something more than physics being involved, the contribution of the Rt. Hon. General Smuts to a discussion on *The Evolution of the Universe* (Britt. Assoc. 1931) is worth quoting. Referring to the view a philosopher might take of the recent discoveries in science, he said:

". . . the physicists, working merely with their own tools and their own incomparable technique and looking for no more than the metrical units which subtend this universe, have indeed, like the man who looked for asses and found a king, found much more than they have looked for. The units they have discovered will constitute not only a world of physics but, in the end and at far removes, also a world of life and spirit. . . .

" These units, particularly the electron and quantum, have an almost meta-physical aspect: they are physics infected with thought. . . .

" Thus it comes that the ultimate units are not purely physical or material but point to an undifferentiated primitive world matrix which includes both the physical and thought characters of the world."

" An undifferentiated primitive world matrix "—surely here is a finely intuitive grasp and understanding of a vast truth.

# CHAPTER IV

## MAN AND THE ELEMENTAL KINGDOMS

THE Web, described in the last chapter, is viewed as the field or basic structure in which all involutionary and evolutionary processes take place. The great waves of Life from the Solar Logos, pregnant with the urge towards manifestation in form, are called during their first three stages of descent " elemental kingdoms ". The relation of these three kingdoms to those which are further advanced, such as the mineral and plant, is shown on diagram No. 10. The first elemental kingdom, shown as at the formless level, from our point of view is quite homogeneous in its nature though bearing within it a pulsing, driving urge towards formal experience.*

The life of the second elemental kingdom, represented in the same chart as on the way down to the third and the mineral kingdom, is best viewed as an almost undifferentiated ocean of consciousness with the divine urge to achieve separation into units aflame within it. Its field, that is its habitat and home, is the Web associated with our earth. Its primary and impelling function is to seize any and every opportunity afforded to enclose a movement within the Web with an envelope that will veil the agitation off from the undifferentiated ocean, and then to appropriate the isolated portion and intensify its life. Thus the elemental life is enabled to acquire a temporary abode for independent experiences. A form, any sort or shape of form, is its never-ceasing quest.

---

* As the human kingdom is the only other that touches the same level it is humanity only that is able adequately to assist the first elemental kingdom to descend. Every high inspiration to which human expression is given in concrete mental terms also aids the first elemental kingdom. The benefit is mutual though the goal of each kingdom is very different.

Number Ten

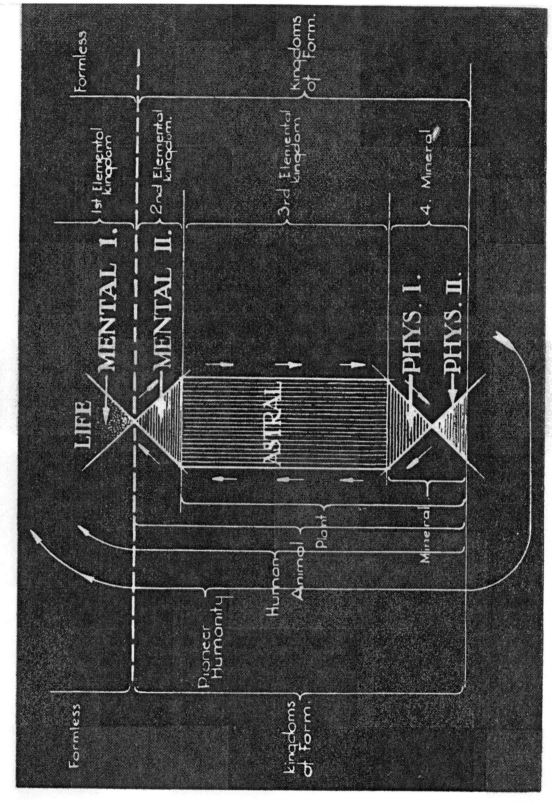

KINGDOMS OF NATURE, ELEMENTAL TO MAN

# MAN AND THE ELEMENTAL KINGDOMS

The purpose of this diagram is to show the inter-relations of the kingdoms of nature and the field covered by each. The formless world of Life is shown as above the horizontal line marking the middle of the mental plane. The first elemental kingdom (the name given to Life at the higher mental level before consciousness or awareness is born) and developed humanity are the only two kingdoms that share this. Life there is represented in the diagram by points of light. Passing across the bridge (the cross at the middle of the mental plane described in Chapter III), Life enters the second elemental kingdom of the lower mental plane, the subtlest part of the three-fold world of form. The descent is continued, as shown by the arrows, to the third elemental kingdom and on to the turning point of the whole vast cycle, the mineral kingdom. With the stabilising assistance of dense physical bodies Life becomes more and more consciously *aware* as it passes through plant and animal forms and acquires astral and mental bodies in addition to the physical. In the human kingdom these three personal bodies are more or less well defined and self-consciousness is achieved. The difficult task now before man is that of establishing self-consciousness at the higher mental level and, with it, the realisation of his true nature.

Throughout, a pioneer humanity few in number and, during the earlier stages not of our own human hierarchy, lead the way.

On the evolutionary cycle, with individuality achieved, man again contacts these elemental kingdoms, for they use the same planes and material forms as those of which his bodies are made. It is the elemental essence, the life of the first, second and third elemental kingdoms, which supplies him with his mental, astral and physical " elementals ".

Trained by long association with animal bodies in earlier cycles it is the " elemental " which instinctively and with mechanical precision controls the so-called automatic functions of the body such as digestion, circulation, etc.

The mental body of a human being may be likened to the disturbed water around a swimmer in a lake. The water immediately near is thrown into agitation, into small waves, which travel outwards with diminishing force. The disturbed water around the swimmer, though part of the lake and not really, of course, to be separated from it, nevertheless is comparatively in a state of isolated agitation. The water so disturbed well serves to illustrate what is meant by a mental body. This simile is particularly applicable concerning the mental plane because of the reaction as described above of the elemental life. Seizing the opportunity with eagerness it isolates and emphasises the locus of disturbance, and this becomes an enclosed abode, a body, which to human consciousness with mental sight is a perfectly clear mental form.

In the same fashion every thought, itself an electric generation within the limits of the mind-body, tends to become separated, though in the great majority of cases it will be speedily dissipated because of the slightness of motive and consequent lack of stability. But if the same type of thought be repeatedly strengthened it is quite possible and indeed common for the elemental life to achieve a semi-independent department in the mind-body where this specialised activity may remain isolated. The human mind may thus become partitioned within itself, indeed frequently is. Hence the origin of fixed ideas, prejudices, divided personalities, complexes of every kind, which modify and colour anything received that is allied to that department of thought much as tinted glasses colour the light seen.

The emotional element in all such happenings and experiences must be included in our understanding of these phenomena, for the third elemental kingdom of the astral plane, itself one stage nearer its objective, the mineral kingdom, aids and abets its brother the elemental life of the second kingdom (manas) and gains an intense measure of experience itself by sharing the forms so diligently manufactured by the human mind both without and within itself.

In view of the perfectly legitimate drive of these two elemental kingdoms towards separated forms and hence keener experiences, it is obvious that this downward or outward urge

42

of the elemental life of the bodies has to be met and overcome by human consciousness. Humanity, on the upward arc, seeking unity and brotherhood, is in an exceedingly difficult situation. Everything is alive—and the life of the very vehicles he has to use in that upward climb is itself headed in the opposite and downward direction. Man has not only to overcome this contrary motion but has himself to mount by its aid. It is very much as if one were faced with the task of walking up an escalator that was moving down! Doubtless, given a sufficient incentive, such a climb would be managed readily. But the incentive in the case of man has to be evoked from within himself, and even when evoked must be followed by intimate experience and knowledge to become compelling. An understanding of the meaning of Good and Evil can arise in those who grapple with and solve the problem of man's relation to these elemental forces. Both the elemental life and man are using the mysterious Web, it is their common field, but their objectives are at opposite poles.

Including as it does all human and elemental experience, the emotional and mental content of the Web at large constitutes the equivalent of the term the *racial unconscious* in present day psychology. The individual human consciousness establishes a relationship between itself and the content of the Web through mento-astral activity. This is greatly assisted by the isolating agility of the elementals and by their repetitive habits, which we call automatic thinking. The relationship is thus secured by means of a floating form, the individual's own auric body, which moves freely and easily through the Web. The idea of a relatively fixed shape moving in changing material has been illustrated already by the movement of a twist of string around a pencil. A further illustration is that of the shape given to a quantity of dry leaves and dust by a scurrying wind. The vortex of air is outlined clearly by the rapidly changing particles. So does the auric body of man (his astro-mental body) move through the Web, its shape being determined by his own habitual reactions to his environment.

Whenever the attention of an individual wanes, and ceases to vivify any part of his auric body, this drops away from the field of his immediate conscious perception and becomes more or less unconscious, though still potentially linked to his auric life through the previous contact. This is the personal unconscious, which can be recalled into direct focus, with greater or less difficulty, according to the conditions so much investigated by psycho-therapists.

Light can be thrown upon the intricate nature of the unconscious mind if the constitution of the Web and the play of the individual mind through it are taken into consideration. All beyond the periphery of the personal mind is in the ocean of pulsing life in the Web, and yet can play upon the individual because mento-emotional contacts between the world-mind and the individual consciousness are continually being made at the psychic levels in addition to the familiar sense contacts of physical experience.

Any response, slight or vivid, made by the man's own mental and emotional aura to this surrounding ocean would seem naturally to arise " in his mind " involuntarily. At present physical contact by the senses of hearing, touch, sight, taste and smell alone are easily cognised as external. Yet by a very little cultivation of one's interior mental and emotional faculties, as apart from the physical, the existence of this vast exterior ocean of active thought and emotion can be verified. And in a very interesting manner too, for one needs only to concentrate intently on a particular subject of interest and the mental body becomes tuned in to thought pulses and emotional waves allied to that subject. Distance, though not negligible, is not very marked under these conditions, but results depend apparently on the degree of sensitivity to which the mind is trained. Responding thus to world thought on similar lines and wave-lengths one's knowledge and understanding may expand, theoretically, to an extent that is unlimited or rather, limited only by the content of the world's Web. This exercise is of course something more than mere introspection, more than an exploration of one's own mental content.*

Fortunately, perhaps, extreme sensitivity is difficult to achieve. The world would be a very trying place in which to live were it easy! But the process can be tested amply enough and proved by anyone exercising some perseverance. We all share the world's unconscious mind together.

Similarly but conversely man's individual mind can influence the contents of the Web profoundly. The higher mind with its flashing speed can mould forms in mental material on the responsive and retentive canvas of the Web as readily and easily as the voice modifies the carrier wave from a broadcasting studio. As the beam from a lantern illumines the darkness of night so may the inner light, focused by the higher mind, illumine and clarify the mental atmosphere of the Web. Much of this is however for the future, for thought-power demands the leaven of wisdom and the subtler worlds still await scientific exploration by man.

The separating veil between a man's mental body and the ocean of semi-conscious life composing the second and third elemental kingdoms is both valuable and necessary, but it also contributes a serious obstacle to release. Its value is inestimable during man's earlier incarnations because the veil isolates consciousness and compels concentration and self-awareness. This very virtue tends however later to make for self-assertion, egotism and a generally aggressive attitude if the separative effort of the elemental life is not understood and combated.

The reiterated advice given so constantly in truly occult teachings which urges the cultivation of poise and balance, the well-known middle way of Buddhism, is given partly because the premature breaking down of this protective veil is fraught with danger. Even the thinning of the veil risks

* This state is called meditation " with seed " in the *Patanjali Sutras on Yoga.*

a too easy contact with the numerous thought-forms and emotional surges of the inner planes unless the individual mind is in some measure already controlled. One of the early steps in gaining such control appears to be the achievement of a certain flexibility of mental habit in place of frozen fixities, followed by the development of deliberately self-chosen thinking. One's mind then responds to and entertains thoughts and feelings only of one's very own choosing. This is an extremely difficult task because of the intense activity of the elemental life both within and without the personal veil. "As hard to curb as the wind", exclaimed Arjuna of the *Bhagavad Gita*, and all who try it are inclined to echo his complaint!

But one immense consolation at least emerges from a study and appreciation of the mysteries of the Web—it is that the normal condition of the Web is static. It is not the' instrument that is responsible for annoyance or pleasure but the player. It is not the basic fabric that we have to control but a fellow-user, to wit, the second elemental kingdom, another traveller, one moreover who is destined to become the most obliging and obedient servant conceivable and a marvellously skilful craftsman under the creative direction of man. The relationship between humanity and the elemental kingdoms may become similar to that between a highly skilled conductor and a finely trained orchestra.

The relation of the higher mind to the lower has been described as resembling that between a pencil point and paper —the pencil point being formless yet capable of building form. This relationship is so true that we must pursue it further. The activity of the higher mental is in fact and deed the activity of a point, a focused point of light. The appropriated atom of the mental plane, called the mental permanent atom, is as a lens, a flashing centre of activity, focusing the buddhic ray of light from the monad. When a human being is on the way to a re-incarnation the field of force playing within the Web assembles a mental sheath or body, which body tends to limit and concentrate the range of the permanent atom and slow down its tremendous natural speed. But however highly organised that appropriated mental body may become, throughout all incarnations and all experiences the egoic mental centre remains in itself a free though focused point of light. This remains true no matter how successful may be its identification with bodies and a personality.

The identification of the point of mental consciousness with its forms is really and merely a deeply printed illusion of consciousness, an illusion that has to be transcended at long last in the human kingdom by the *self*-imposed discipline of meditation. As a focus of buddhic light, and hence of the very nature of light, the higher mental centre can move with the speed of light. This terrific speed is the main obstacle to be overcome in the change from life to consciousness, from mere life at large to life aware that it *is* alive. Therefore the value of the Web, the net, in which the souls of men are caught, as Egyptian symbology has it.

The limitations imposed and the privations experienced in the forms of the personality built in the Web compel comparatively slow and ponderous responses. The privations at length achieve the purpose set: life passes into consciousness (awareness) and consciousness into self-awareness until, in humanity, as more and more freedom is achieved, release from the illusions imposed by forms becomes possible.

From these illusions it is however desperately difficult entirely to escape. The active higher mental centre is by now so supremely skilful in the art of producing forms easily and readily in the responsive medium of its department of the Web that to withdraw, consciously to withdraw, from the mentally complexed net is exceedingly hard. For that matter, in terms of the greater cycles and the unfoldment of the powers latent in human consciousness, this achievement of withdrawal is a task quite legitimately to be achieved in future cycles by the vast majority. But it can undoubtedly be done now. The physical world for humanity is already objective, the physical body itself is becoming objective; release from identification with the astral and mental bodies will render them objective too and the self can then be realised as spirit.

Karma, usually translated as the law of cause and effect, reaction to action, becomes now more readily understandable. Every personal activity in the Web, whether mental, emotional or physical, modifies the corresponding vibrational measure of the Web, the tattva of the plane. And the law is that every such modification is subtly and indissolubly connected with its creator until unravelled and dissipated. Skandhas, as they are called, are simple or severe distortions in the Web, held intact and separate by the eager elemental life, which by their very origin and nature are tuned in to their creator and tend to react on him. Action and reaction are equal and opposite and the fruits of his personal action may be either " good " or " bad ". Strain or distortion is occasioned if there be any element of personal attachment to the thought, feeling or deed. It may be of trifling moment or strongly impressed, easily rectified or of long duration. Only in the case of action initiated utterly selflessly, that is, with no hooking back of the interest or intention upon its creator, is there no magnetic tie—and that means that the motive is buddhic, i.e., it has its origin in the universal consciousness, and such an action is that of a Saviour.*

Yet personally motived action, with a full content of selfish acquisitiveness, has its indispensable place in the early stages of human consciousness to ensure that the mental and emotional bodies shall be well defined and rigidly limited, in order firmly to foster and establish clear cut individualisation. Hence the succession of legitimate incentives cited in the ancient laws of conduct for the four castes: (1) Sensory Pleasure, (2) Wealth, (3) Fame, (4) Service.

Unless individuality be thoroughly well-founded there is

---

* " Having abandoned attachment to the fruit of action . . . *he is not doing* anything although doing actions." *Bhag. Gita* 4.20.

48

apt to be an absence of personal incentive, few " mistakes " and little real experience. The Satanic Hierarchy, the mighty Asuras, fortunately have successfully guarded against many failures arising from this cause among our own human hierarchy by the intensity with which individual consciousness has been developed under their tutelage, but their very success has bred a momentum from which we find it hard in this cycle to attain release.

## CHAPTER V

## CONSCIOUSNESS AND THE DIMENSIONS OF SPACE

ENTERING on the cycles of involution and evolution, Life in the first instance alights at the junction-point portals of the Web and then proceeds to explore and annex its new and entrancing territory. The procession through the kingdoms of form is led by skilled human pioneers who, on the previous Chain of Globes, had had experience in form mastery. A new land, the dense physical world, has in the course of this Chain to be entered, inhabited and mastered, as also the already familiar corridor of approach through the lower mental, the astral and the etheric.

The mineral, plant and animal forms, built up during vastly extensive periods of time, permit life to apprehend the three dimensions of space *in succession*. Indeed not till the true archetypal form of the human being is attained is the whole of spatial extension embraced.

To understand this mystery it is necessary to pause here and consider the problem of consciousness in relation to the dimensions of space. Forms are built from a centre outwards —the first centres to be used being those innumerable junction-points of the Web prepared by Father-Mother. Here life begins its journey through the forms of the kingdoms of nature and spends the whole of the first Round in achieving the unit of organised form—the cell. In the second Round the cell has become the unit of form growth as the result of the inter-play of the third and second Aspects of the Solar Logos. Though there is a deal of overlapping, for life knows no absolute boundaries, we may take it that the mineral form is dominant in the first Round, the plant form in the second and the animal form in the third. In the fourth Round, the present one, the human form is at length achieved—though not as we know it till the third and fourth Races of our own world occupation.

The building and establishment of the earlier kingdoms is described therefore in Theosophical literature as having taken the first three Rounds of our Chain to accomplish—and even they are held to be comparatively rapid recapitulations of the vast work of the first three Chains. When in the fourth Round our world was reached, the first three Root-Races again rapidly recapitulated the work of the three earlier Rounds, hence not till the fourth Race was reached on the earth was positively new work undertaken. And in the fourth Race, following the successful and long-prepared-for " descent " of the human form, the whole three-dimensional world of the mental, astral and physical planes is at length, through the elaborate mechanism of the truly human being, for the first time within Life's grasp.

That the succession of the kingdoms described above and the final arrival of human consciousness in a human form may be clearly followed it will be useful to trace the successive advances made by Life through the forms of the kingdoms to its ultimate victory over the so-called three dimensions of space. Incidentally the real meaning of what is meant by a fourth dimension may emerge.

By the term *dimensions of space* we really mean *extensions of matter*, and if we analyse this latter term we shall resolve it into motion of a point or points—motion in three directions that we call height, breadth, and depth. These popularly are the three dimensions of space and mathematically, not actually, may be regarded as arising in succession—height being due to the motion of a point in one direction, which we call a line; breadth being due to the motion of this line at right angles to itself, which we call a surface; and depth being the movement of this surface, again at right angles to itself, which we call a solid. These are the three dimensions.

51

The fourth dimension theory is that there may be a further movement at right angles to the three-dimensional solid figure, a movement or extension obviously not possible to trace, but nevertheless, it has been claimed, following as a natural, reasonable and logical sequence to the first three movements. A wealth of delightful and fascinating analogies has been built up on the imagined relations of the inhabitants of flatland, i.e., a two-dimensional world with those of a one-dimensional world on the one hand and our three-dimensional world on the other. The theory has the air of being based on the essence of sound reasoning; it is attractive, explanatory, and at first somewhat captivating. Yet is it none the less misleading and fallacious, for it is an attempt to identify the attributes of Life with the figures of Form and, however willingly we grant that behind the words fourth dimension there stands something that is real, it is of importance that that reality should be described in terms of Life or consciousness and not be regarded as a further extension of matter or Form. ("Time" in this connection is another story.)

Without pausing to inquire what becomes of the fundamental simplicity of the unity on which the Universe is based if dimensions are multiplied *ad infinitum*, let us examine briefly the popular argument. The approach to the imaginary fourth dimension by its advocates is usually by way of the first, second and third. The reader is introduced to an imaginary linear world and then to a flatland of two dimensions, described in detail and with much ingenuity, and thus on to our own familiar world the land of solids. By the help of numerous analogies the student is instructed to attempt a conception of a four-dimensional world. At first sight all the difficulty appears to reside only in this last effort, but a little thought will convince one that the linear world and flatland are just as impossible of conception! In terms of form they can themselves have no independent existence. To picture flatland the reader is invited to imagine a plane surface with paper squares and triangles upon it, or smooth water with the thinnest of films moving over it. Quite a comfortably easy task, but it is not flatland because all such superimposed divisions involve at once a third dimension.

A three-dimensional world of form is indeed the only one conceivable, for a line is the boundary of a surface and has no existence apart from a surface; a surface is the boundary of a solid and has no existence apart from a solid. The solid form contains the three dimensions, and all manifest not successively but together, springing equally and simultaneously full-grown from the Creative Source, for they correspond to the triune nature of the One Life, to the triple attributes of every unity.

Now consider the relation of Life to Form and we shall readily understand the succession of the dimensions in terms of consciousness and what is meant by the fourth factor.

Life enters the threefold form world impelled, first, to respond to it through the vehicle adopted—achieving consciousness, awareness, in the process—and then to master it. Life may be depicted on the preliminary formless level as centred in nuclei or points of pure being (jivas) whose Will-to-live finds its field of expression in Form—for all that may be encountered within the ring-pass-not of the form worlds is to be rendered subject to that Will. These points of Being become units of consciousness on meeting the resistance offered by material, though the growth of the quality of awareness is slow.

The whole journey may be regarded as accomplished in seven stages and the succession is best expounded with the help of diagram No. 11.

(A) On the threshold of the Form World. Life is diagrammatically represented as a point, " Will ", which is about to commence its experiences. The point is localised in the junction of the cross which itself is at the foundation of the form worlds. Alighting here life has its first experience of consciousness or awareness by reason of the resistance offered by

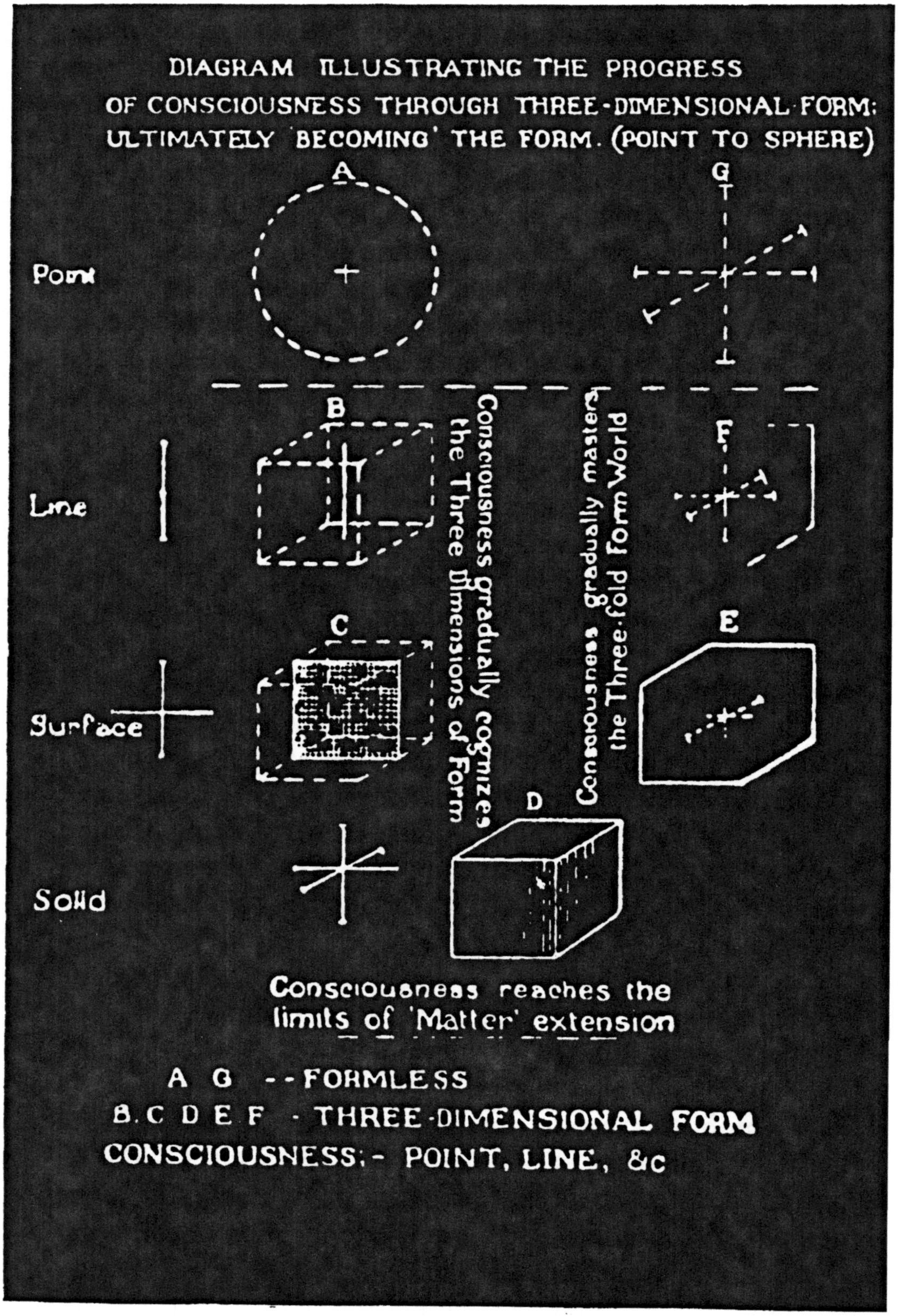

DIAGRAM ILLUSTRATING THE PROGRESS
OF CONSCIOUSNESS THROUGH THREE-DIMENSIONAL FORM:
ULTIMATELY BECOMING THE FORM. (POINT TO SPHERE)

A

G

Point

B

Line

Consciousness gradually cognizes
the Three Dimensions of Form

Consciousness gradually masters
the Three-fold Form World

F

C

Surface

E

D

Solid

Consciousness reaches the
limits of 'Matter' extension

A G --FORMLESS
B.C D E F · THREE-DIMENSIONAL FORM
CONSCIOUSNESS:- POINT, LINE, &c

Number Eleven

the veil of matter.  Position is achieved, little else.  Concious-
ness is of the slightest—for " God sleeps in the Mineral ".
This slight consciousness however means a probing in the
three directions or extensions of matter and hence the begin-
nings of mineral form—centres, axes of vibration, geometrical
activity.  Life in the mineral kingdom has attained localisa-
tion or position and some, but very little, conscious extension.
Hence its symbol is the point—that which has position but no
magnitude.

(B)  Continuing its excursion and succeeding in definitely
appropriating an extension along a single line, the pioneering
Life identifies itself with it and senses one dimension: that
is, it becomes conscious by its ability, through a single line as
a vehicle, to respond slightly to one mode of motion.  This is
linear consciousness and the kingdom of which this is typical
is the vegetable.  We may trace this to-day in the vegetable
life which, starting from a centre (seed), clothes itself in a form
that strikes down and up.  Through the earlier progress of
this kingdom these thrusting extremities of root, stem and
branches, traversing one dimension, may be regarded as the
sensitive organs of plant consciousness.

(C)  The third stage, C in the chart, corresponds to animal
consciousness, to which two dimensions are objective.  Consciousness is feeling its way forward, living the more keenly
as sensation increases.  Sensation awakens desire and aversion
and these enhance experience so that consciousness tends continually to identify itself more thoroughly with its instrument
of sensation.  The visual organ of the animal body presents
consciousness with only a flat picture and, as the average
animal is unaided by any considerable mental development,
perception must necessarily be limited to height and breadth
—the conscious outlook being thus practically superficial.
The diagram therefore depicts this consciousness as two-
dimensional.

(D)  In the next period of development the three dimensions
are apprehended by virtue of the development of mentality

—height, breadth and depth begin in a measure to be all objective. Self-consciousness becomes established as the human form, held at the archetypal level in the Divine Mind, is projected outward and descends into formal manifestation. Life in the human kingdom responds to the three modes of motion, embraces the three dimensions, functions through three vehicles, effects relations with the whole of the threefold world of form and is enabled thereby to distinguish between its own densest vehicle and others. This achieved awareness of isolation from other forms spells self-apprehension. The unit of consciousness itself remains always as a living *point* only and is engaged throughout the outward journey (in the diagram, A, B, C and half-way through D) in becoming acquainted and identified with the three-dimensional world of form, learning through its appropriated and intimate vehicle to vibrate in sympathy with its environment. It is essential to remember that it is awareness, consciousness, that progresses through the form dimensions and not the forms themselves—*they* are, strictly speaking, always three-dimensional.

At this periphery of the form-worlds the attention of the unit of Consciousness is devoted to externals, i.e., to the environment. This is the inevitable result of the long and successful training received in its journey from the point stage to an apprehension of the three-dimensional solid, throughout which the spiritual urge has been outwards. Broadly speaking, this is the position of humanity to-day. The return journey has now to be undertaken for, after the critical self-conscious stage is successfully established following the apprehension of the threefold world, there follows the task of mastery and subjection. "Matter must become the obedient servant of the Spirit."

(E) We come now to the crucial part of this exposition, for this step is the first on the return journey and corresponds to that usually associated with a fourth dimension—erroneously so called, for the process is clearly one involving the partial mastery of our three-dimensional world of the three planes and is not a further excursion of consciousness through another extension of form.

To appreciate this stage it is necessary to pause in order first to understand clearly the mechanism involved in sense-response. Let us take the sense of sight as typical. On the physical level we " see " because the retina of the eye responds to light and shade. It is this reproduction made by our appropriated vehicle that enables us to see and, if we examine it, we shall find that the visual reproduction amounts only to a picture in two dimensions, and even this is due entirely to light reflected from the surface of the object. So much for the mechanical process which represents but a part of the art of " seeing ". To this part the man applies his mentality and having by its means acquired three-dimensional perception at once interprets the simple picture in terms of perspective, imposing depth by the action of his mind. In other words the retinal picture is reproduced in the mind body, a material vehicle as already described, and displayed there in three dimensions; and moreover the object is seen, not by means of an external light, projecting a flat picture only, but by virtue of its own luminosity. At present the vast majority of humanity see the exterior of the object only, but actually the content of the whole is reproduced, for the *interior* of the three-dimensional image presented is *within the mind too.*

The point of Consciousness, which is the true man, plays freely within his own vehicle and can view this image in any part or as a whole at will. The measure of his training will determine the accuracy of the reproduction and the value of his perception. In the process of developing interior sight there are certain to be many errors of reading. The standpoint assumed by a trained consciousness wherefrom to view such a reproduction within the subtle vehicle of his own mind is naturally the centre—and the whole interior of the image is displayed to such a consciousness at once. Front, back, sides

57

and interior are all equally perceived and hence there is abundant possibility of confusion and misunderstanding. Nature provides, however, a valuable corrective, which saves the situation. Just as in the physical eye there is a minute spot on the retina affording intense focal definition, the enormous benefits of which by the way we hardly appreciate, so in the astro-mental vehicle there is a centre of special visual sensitiveness. Playing through this localised centre Consciousness gains clarity at the cost of some limitation—a cost very well worth incurring. For instead of attempting the impossible task of grasping the three dimensions at once, as might be inferred, Consciousness masters one dimension at a time. It *becomes* itself depth, so to speak, by virtue of the flashing speed of the " point " of life, and thus senses everything displayed in terms of two dimensions. Hence in the diagram (*E*) Consciousness is shown as *being* the dotted line (depth) and as seeing objectively only breadth and height. This *becoming* means in practical terms that the higher mental point of consciousness responds to the whole of depth very rapidly and yet consciously. The so-called fourth-dimensional Consciousness is really a return to two-dimensional objectivity with the acquisition of one dimension mastered. Consciousness in short has *become* a third part of its environment and can reproduce this third correctly, instantaneously and completely at will.

(*F*) The next step, the mastery of another dimension—breadth, is perhaps rather difficult to follow intellectually, though a simple illustration will assist, for at this step two dimensions become consciously assimilated, one only remaining objective. Take a page of print and hold it so as to foreshorten it to extreme by looking almost at the bottom edge; the whole of the text of many lines will be foreshortened apparently into one line—one dimension. The experiment faintly suggests stage F if it be further supposed that the expanded consciousness can read the whole page as if it were the one line. At this stage two dimensions will have been mastered and form phenomena may be comprehended in one synthetic dimension only.

(*G*) Consciousness at this stage is represented as having taken the final step of the series. Three dimensions are now mastered and the formless level is again attained. The units of life are responsive to all within the limits of the ring-pass-not, they are masters of all the forms of the threefold world, they can consciously move at the same or a greater speed than can material and hence can embrace within themselves all the possibilities of the three extensions of matter. The Points in this sense are omnipresent and hence have become the Sphere.

Consciousness is thus shown as having traced its way through the kingdoms, encountering and grappling with the resistances of worlds of form, apprehending their threefold character in successive stages. At the limit of its outward sweep Consciousness achieves awareness of itself and proceeds to the mastery of Forms in similar successive stages, inversely this time, by transmuting their extensions into conscious interior experience.

CHAPTER VI

## MAN'S ORIGINS

THE theory that Man is the product and capital of an end-on evolutionary column, rising in a more or less sequential series from earlier kingdoms of nature, held the field in the nineteenth century. Though challenged now from many angles, particularly from the results of biological and anatomical research, the theory has not yet given place in the popular mind to any other as acceptable nor to anything seemingly so well founded. Yet the many theoretical structures, based on the facts and inferences of Lamarck's and Darwin's works, have been found wanting, indeed no wholly satisfactory edifice has arisen from them.

In the *Secret Doctrine*, published in 1889, Mme. Blavatsky challenged the current theories. She wrote :

"The esoteric teaching is absolutely opposed to the Darwinian evolution, as applied to man, and partially so with regard to other species." *S.D. II, p.* 689.

"That man was not the last member of the mammalian family, but the first in this Round, is something that Science will be forced to acknowledge one day." *II, p.* 164.

"The Occult Doctrine maintains that the mammalians were a later work of evolution than man." *II, p.* 190.

"Man has been on earth, in this Round, from the beginning." *II, p.* 265.

This is a revolutionary view to-day even though in every other theory of man's origin many flaws have been found and exposed.

That the ape is descended from man, is indeed decadent man, has long been suspected though the more widely held view still is that man and ape derive from a common stock.

60

Mme. Blavatsky's statements are far more searching. If they can be shown to be even theoretically sound a vista opens to the sources of human origins which may well deserve the term spiritual. Their revolutionary character need not deter us in view of the many reversals of opinion that already have been adopted.

Consider for a moment the reversals we consistently have made as consciousness functions in an increasing measure at the higher mental level and hence becomes more detached from the forms immediately at hand. It is a commonplace of modern psychology that when an unconscious condition is genuinely externalised and we see ourselves definitely as separate from it all its values tend to be altered. So in the history of human thought. As we have developed the capacity for larger views, concepts based on previous experiences frequently have had to be reversed. The flat earth of our early personal judgment, for instance, has long become a sphere; our planet is not, as once was vigorously believed, stationary and geocentric but circles round the sun; the consciousness of a child is not now regarded as an empty vessel requiring to be filled so much as an abounding treasure-house needing release; medical treatment and healing generally are becoming more and more an interior mental and emotional art, concerned with psychological processes, in place of a purely exterior physical science; the penal code is beginning to recognise the need for education in place of mere reprisal; the very Deity is vacating the distant skies for the heart of man; —these and many other reversals are evidences of the rectification of earlier errors as our view-point advances. To reverse the position of man on the evolutionary ladder and place him on the top-most rung, precedent to any form-manifestation as we know it, may well prove to be the solution of the many problems relating to his origin.

The occult teaching in its broadest application is indeed that man himself represents the archetype whence all nature's forms derive.

Almost in these words H.P.B. sums up her views on human origins. In one passage, after lengthy references to many ancient myths, sagas and legends, most of them claimed to be concerned with the same mystery teaching, she states:

". . . all have an identical meaning and relate to the primordial Archetypal Man, the Creative Origin of all things."
*S.D., Vol. I, p.* 478.
and—". . . these represent primarily the Archetypal Man, the Protologos." p. 380.

A note here is necessary respecting the application of the term Man. It is used in the *Secret Doctrine* to include a great deal more than a human being as we know him. To-day *man* is our own fourth Creative Hierarchy and wears the familiar human form. To the occult student the term *man* denotes a state of consciousness and not a particular form. The man of any period is given this title because he performs a particular function, that of bridging the highest forces contacted in that cycle to the lowest. In the chart that follows an attempt is made to show the work of the various humanities or Creative Hierarchies of the four Chains already manifested in our Solar System. From this it will be seen that the forms used by each humanity are the pioneer experiment of the Chain: once achieved they are thrown off by the pioneer and used by less evolved types of consciousness. The successful humanity of the period moves on to other creative efforts.

This chart shows the relation between members of the human kingdom and the forms used on the four Chains of our Scheme. It is said that, though the greater number of a successful humanity from a Chain of globes may pass on to other spheres of activity, a part elects to stay and assist the Life of the succeeding Chains and fill particular Offices in their government, as Asuras, etc.

# MAN'S ORIGINS

## CHAIN I

Part of the humanity of this Chain are now the Asura Hierarchy and three kingdoms in advance of our own human kingdom.

Mineral like forms were made and inhabited by pioneer humanity on the mental plane.

On the phys. plane of our world similar forms are densified and now inhabited by mineral life.
(Illus. No. 13.)

## CHAIN II

Part of this humanity are now the Agnishvatta Hierarchy and two kingdoms in advance of ours.

Plant like forms were made and inhabited by pioneer humanity on the astral plane.

On the phys. plane of our world similar forms are densified and now inhabited by vegetable life.
(Illus. Nos. 15 and 16.)

## CHAIN III

Part of this humanity are now the Barhishad Hierarchy and one kingdom in advance of ours.

Animal like forms were made and inhabited by pioneer humanity on the etheric plane.

On the phys. plane of our world similar forms are densified and now inhabited by reptilian animal life.

## CHAIN IV

Our present day humanity.

Human forms were made and inhabited on the current Round IV. From the earliest and subtlest of human forms it is said that our mammalia are all derived.

During its first three Rounds this Chain recapitulated rapidly the work of the 3 preceding Chains. On Round IV all types of forms reach the physical plane.

The above classification does not imply that there are any sharply defined boundaries, for allowance must be made for the wide divergencies and overlapping demanded by the Life. As the archetypal human form gradually descended from the higher mental plane to the dense physical frequent advances were made far beyond the forms related to the Chain cycles above. On Chain III for instance it is said that human forms on the etheric plane and verging on the dense physical were achieved by advanced human beings of that Chain. The above chart should be taken as indicating averages only.

The statement that man stands at the head of the stream of life, is the origin himself of nature's forms, is indeed startling, yet a familiar analogy gives point and reason to this view. An architect, in process of designing a building, mentally pictures a plan and an elevation, with their embellishments, and then reduces these three-dimensional conceptions to the symbols of line and colour on two-dimensional paper. Various craftsmen then interpret the design given and embody it in physical material. The mental creation comes first, then the design symbolised in line and curve, then the edifice. The architect begins his projection into objectivity by creation on the mental level, and the mental forms, three-dimensional on their own plane, are as objective there as the finished building is in the physical world.

Thought of this nature always precedes physical action and the occult student recognises that such deliberately created mental forms are as independently real and self-contained in the architect's mental field as the later construction in stone and timber is in the physical world. All this, of course, may be applied to the creative activity of every artist whatever his medium. One point in this analogy needs specially to be stressed and that is that the artist's mental creation is of the nature of an archetype. This means that it is an original type or form-pattern from which certain structures may be projected by action. Experiments or try-outs with the structure in a physical medium, whether the artist be architect, painter, poet or musician, will result in many modifications, many changes, till the artist achieves some measure of success in portraying an aspect of his creation. Whatever the final result the archetype is the mental model from which the result is derived and is the cause of its appearance, though a host of such projected exhibits may be needed adequately to manifest the original archetype.

The application of this analogy is far reaching, but there is probably little need to labour it for the sequence of mental conception to physical expression is within the experience of all and quite familiar. Substitute for the architect in our analogy a Super-Being who, having conceived of a solar system and carried it into manifestation to the stage of a thought-form of our world, constructs in thought a living miniature of his own creative capacities, namely archetypal man, to serve as a progenitor for the living forms of that world—and we have a picture somewhere near the theory submitted.

A diagram displaying the successive stages of descent of the archetype and its successful projection at the fourth stage will assist in following this sequence.

Let us now look a little more closely at the forms built and used as bodies by the human hierarchies of the earlier Chains.

The first globe to be manifested in form was, as already shown (Chart No. 2), of mental material, based on the Web and serving the purpose of a planetary mind. This was the field wherein manifestation began, for it provided the mirror in which subjective Life could reflect itself as objective Form. Life, or Light, became focused therein. It is arrested by this fabric and gyrates, flashing from focused centres along radii and around orbits.

The numbers 1 to 7 indicate the seven successive Rounds of our Chain. Archetypal man is shown as gradually achieving clear re-presentation in physical material. In Round I the form that we now call the mineral was established by pioneer man at the mental level and was the dominant factor in that Round. In Round II the plant form at the astral level was the most significant form. In Round III similarly the animal up to and including the reptilian type, at the etheric level, was the focal experiment. In Round IV the erect human form in physical material is established, and is maintained through the next three Rounds till the end of the Chain. Solar energy plays continuously from above and, after Round II, lunar and terrene energy from below. The centres awakened and localised in the physical body, itself a synthesis of the whole, are named in the last column of the diagram.

In the fourth Round it follows that the 1st, 2nd, 3rd and 4th Root-Races of our current world occupation were rapid recapitulations of the completed work of the earlier Rounds. Hence the figures 5, 6, 7, symbolising the later Rounds, must be understood as indicating developments very much of the future, and successfully to be achieved, for the majority of our human race, only in the 5th, 6th and 7th *Rounds* respectively, hence not on this globe in the present Round except by the adventurous few. Our 5th, 6th and 7th Root-Races are and will be merely brief rehearsals of the great play set to be staged in the last three Rounds.

Number Thirteen

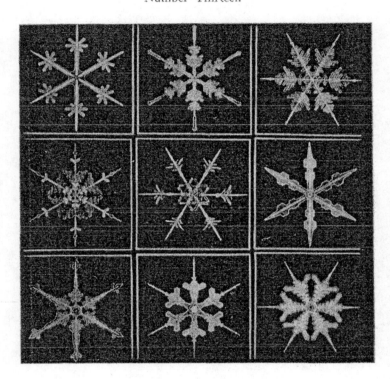

VARIETIES OF ICE CRYSTALS

Number Twelve

Number Fourteen

### SOUND FIGURES PRODUCED BY THE VOICE

Geometrical figures, outlined in sand, produced by the vibration of a glass or rubber disc will be familiar to many. A violin bow drawn across the edge of a glass plate or the human voice sounded into a vessel covered with rubber sheeting are the usual means employed to obtain the effects illustrated in No. 14 above. Mrs. Watts Hughes, many years since, carried out some fascinating experiments in the production of such forms with the voice, in sand or fine powder, as also in a semi-fluid medium. The above reproduction of voice figures and the beautiful tree form, No. 22, are from her monograph, *Eidophone Voice Figures*. The form building power of the waves of sound which can be generated by the human voice is in close illustration of the relation of Life to Form, of the Cosmic Breath to the fabric of the Web. The resemblance of these voice-built forms to crystal and plant structures is very striking and lends significance and meaning to the many occult references to the voice as being the real creative agent.

The Sons of Light referred to in the *Stanzas of Dzyan* were human monads, and their first vahan or body, built in the first Chain, we should now describe as having the form of the mineral kingdom, with centres, angles, axes, etc., first constructed in a purely mental world on the first and simplest plan.

Though astral and physical worlds and bodies have since been added to the mental, we still, as humans, originate thought on these same principles.  In the course of the cycles we have registered innumerable experiences in the spark-like centres of the mentally active Web which still consistently arrests and reflects our life.  At the touch of our attention these centres light up in our mental bodies and re-display to us as spectators the scenes and incidents there registered, and we say " I remember " this or that.  The memory-lag of the Web resembles the vision-lag of the retina of the eye, though much more durable.

Thought-forms, humanly created, are based on these centres and axes of growth and expand or fade as the light of our attention ensouls them or is withdrawn.  Mental propagation is somewhat analogous to fission, for telepathy tends to excite in another's mind the same form or feeling as is experienced by the producer—an occurrence, by the way, which is much more frequent than is supposed.  Our physical means of communication corresponding to this is, at present, almost exclusively by the use of language and the pen.  The British Broadcasting Company provides an excellent example of propagation on mental lines though here the medium and mechanism are at the etheric and physical level.  Each active receiving set reproduces the original " thought " exactly as thrown out—unless the receiver is faulty, as many a human mind is, and then the original form is distorted proportionally.

The first adumbration of archetypal man is thus seen achieving position in the Web—little more.  Man is no-dimensional at this stage.  " A dimensionless image " Mme.

Blavatsky calls him. (*Vol. I, p.* 199.) As pioneer he establishes and endows centres and radii, and passes on, leaving his footsteps to guide and assist the younger life to follow. The mineral form is thus founded.

In the second Chain the Sons of Light, a humanity two generations earlier than ourselves, had their chief centre of activity on the astral globe, in addition to the mental, of that Chain. A clothing of fluidic material with membrane and envelope is assembled. The plant form appears and a medium for feeling and warm emotion is added to the mechanism of cold thinking.

The circulatory and lymphatic systems of the later physical human body are adumbrated at this stage, for in the early plant forms of the mento-astral worlds vascular structure is achieved. The astral world is of such a nature as to permit of

Number Fifteen

CELL OF THE HUMAN CEREBRAL CORTEX

the projection of the fluidic circulatory system inherent in the archetype.

Number Sixteen

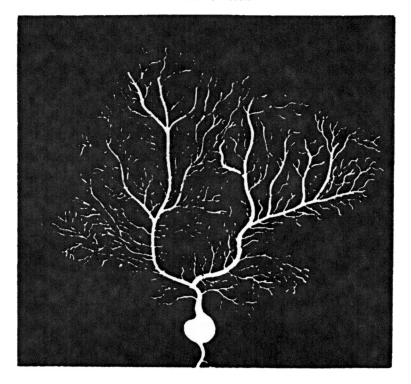

CELL FROM THE HUMAN CEREBELLUM
From *Halliburton's Physiology*

Man's nervous and circulatory systems are obviously suggestive, on the form side, of plant growths. Roots are represented by the brain and stem and foliage by the spinal cord with its extensions and proliferations. All these are of the plant type in construction. Coupled with the ancient occult symbol of the Ashvattha-Tree, with roots in the heavens and foliage on earth, the " reversed " direction of the nervous structure is significant, for it suggests in itself man's " descent " from the heights. That man in the second Round, by building forms in the astral and etheric media, set the pattern of vegetable processes and hence was their originator and creator, is the theory here advanced. The life of the younger kingdom, following in man's steps, adopted the forms and elaborated and specialised them as they " descended " and hardened into the denser physical medium.

70

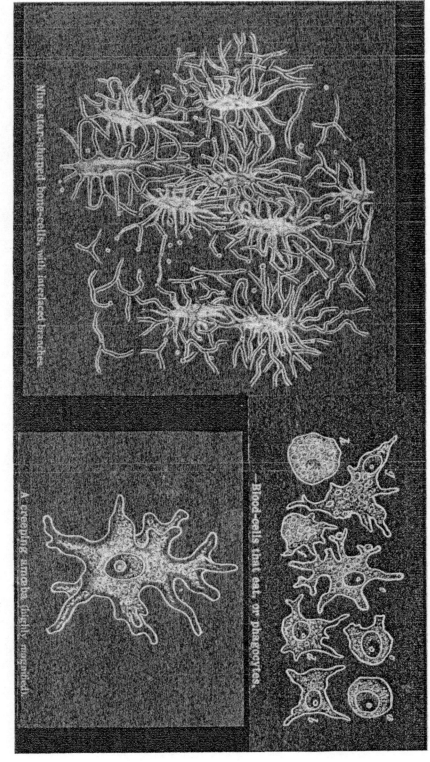

Number Seventeen

Nine star-shaped bone-cells, with interlaced branches.

Number Nineteen

A creeping amoeba (highly magnified).

Number Eighteen

Blood-cells that eat, or phagocytes.

The resemblance of the single-celled amoeba, one of the simplest of animal forms, to the cells of the human body whether in the fixed structure of bone or the fluid medium of the blood, is very apparent in the illustrations above. All organised physical bodies are built of cell units.

The implication of the foregoing is therefore that the physical human form as we know it must be regarded itself as the direct representative of the " creative origin of all things ". The physical body of man is, even to-day, compared with many plant and animal forms, simple, unextended, unspecialised. Nevertheless it contains within itself every potentiality. Not till the physical plane is reached and the fourth hierarchy, our own, is in action, is the archetypal form brought right through and projected in the outermost world of our Solar Scheme.

In each Cycle it is the human archetypal form, manifesting successively on the mental, astral and etheric planes, whence all other forms derive.

In the earlier Rounds and Cycles of our Solar Scheme it was the preceding hierarchies of humanity who played the archetypal part. Propagation was by methods of fission on the mental globe, by budding on the astral world and by sweatborn extrusion in the etheric (moon) period. These remain the characteristic methods of mineral, plant and some animal forms to-day. During the cycles mentioned it must be noted that the human form, the progenitor, is described as composed " of the most tenuous matter compatible with objectivity ".

Thus, as man descended gradually into materiality he periodically threw off from him fragments and essences (the Sanscrit terms are translated into *dust* and *sweat*) which, seized by junior grades of life, were developed along their own specialised lines in plant and animal directions. Ultimately arriving in his own completed physical form, more flexibly constructed and less prone to specialisation than many which had been cast aside, man classifies the animals, plants and minerals as of younger kingdoms of nature.

When thrown off the younger forms tended to materialise comparatively rapidly. As the fragments of hot iron falling in sparks from the smith's forge cool and harden more quickly than the hot bar itself, so the younger life, seizing the extruded substance from the astral and ethereal human frame, cooled and materialised long before man himself did in the physical world. Hence the abundant traces in this world of plant and animal forms prior to those of man.

Number Twenty                                             Number Twenty-one

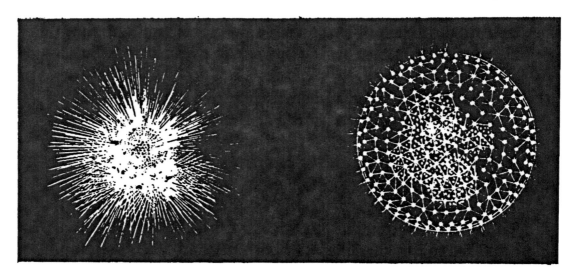

In the development of animal forms a stage resembling a maze of lines branching from a central nucleus is a reminder of the mineral type. An example of such is the illustration of a marine animalcule, the *globigerina*, above. Also a specimen of the open " basket-work " pattern frequently met with in the microscopic life of the pond and stream, the *volvox*. Students will be reminded of the " lines " and " basket-works " description of the higher bodies of man in their early stages. Much of this early work in the building of animal forms was done on the third Chain.

## Man's Relation to the Mammalia

Madame Blavatsky points out that in this Round our own humanity has been the progenitor of mammalian forms. (*S.D. Vol. II*, 164, 265.)

Our humanity, the fourth, has been vastly assisted by standing, so to speak, on the shoulders of the preceding, and it is

Number Twenty-two

A FORM BUILT IN A SEMI-LIQUID MEDIUM
BY THE HUMAN VOICE

ment though not entirely adequate in the view of occultists.*

Other authorities might be cited concerning the non-specialised character of the human body. The tendency to recognise this is quite marked in current thought. For instance, in a B.B.C. talk published in the *Listener*, Nov. 21st 1934, Gerald Heard spoke on the subject *Man, the Non-Specialist*. Mr. Heard pointed out truly enough that man is a tool-using creature and that tool-making has adequately served man in providing clothing, shelter, food produce, locomotion, etc.,—hence he has never needed to specialise his limbs.

The principle enunciated, founded on Man as the archetypal, original model, covers and relates these views and explains much more. Man as the archetype bears within himself the potentiality of all extensions and every user of the human form shares this immense inheritance. Each main division of the mineral, plant and animal kingdoms emerging from the archetypal form at the mental, astral, etheric or dense physical levels, as the case might be, would develop and extend its qualities of specialisation along its own line to the fullest extent of its vital and partially conscious drive. Life, being always the driving urge, builds the forms and extends them each strictly according to the limit of capacity. Each specialised line, bovine, equine, canine, feline, etc., achieves a wholeness determined by its purpose, each elaborating some aspect of the original human form far beyond that needed by the unspecialised and hence ever adaptable human frame.

According therefore to the occult tradition the human signature is to be found on the forms of the kingdoms of nature everywhere. As the archetypal author of all, man has " named " all. His own physical body is a representation in physical terms of the archetypal man; it is a body of com-

* *The Problem of Man's Ancestry*, by F. Wood Jones, Prof. Anatomy, 1918, London University.

paratively simple construction and fitted especially, if it can be said to be specialised at all, to serve as a medium for human thinking. The stable and yet adaptable physical body and the dense world in which man is now functioning enable him to externalise his mental processes by means of the mirror-like Web with precision and so to master them. In this mastery the stupendous powers of mentality may be dis-covered and the spiritual nature of his own life realised.

This is the occult theory of man's origin, reversing the popular conceptions of evolution by placing man as the ancestor, in terms of form, of the mineral, vegetable and animal kingdoms of nature as well as, of course, his own.

> " Occultism teaches that no form can be given to anything whose ideal type does not already exist on the subjective plane . . . our human forms have existed in the Eternity as ethereal prototypes . . . these supersensuous moulds contained, besides their own, the elements of all the vegetable and animal forms of this globe. Therefore, man's outward shell passed through every vegetable and animal body before it assumed the human shape." *S.D., Vol I, p.* 303.

CHAPTER VII

# CREATIVE ENERGY: LUNAR, TERRENE AND SOLAR

W E speak of generating stations and power houses, of the triumphs of industrial machinery, of the invention of high explosives and mighty engines of war—and need occasionally to be reminded that man can create *de novo* no force, no energy, no power whatever. Not one single foot-pound of energy can he in truth create. By the skilful use of nature's elements he can collect and confine existing forces of a certain order and can then distribute the temporarily imprisoned power, such as steam and electricity, along specially prepared channels to do his chosen work. Man can create new forms but never new forces.

Sun, moon and earth provide in exhaustless abundance the power on which he can draw—and by far the larger proportion still remains to be utilised. All is said to be within human reach, for the occult definition of man is that he is the being, in any Chain of globes, who links highest spirit and lowest matter. Adopting this definition it follows that man is the focus and provides the vehicle for forces playing both from lofty heights and deeply involved depths; he stands between two extremes and his task is the building of a bridge which shall span the gulf, a bridge that can be no other than himself in his own perfected consciousness.

The sun, representative in manifestation of the first Aspect of the divine Life, is the source of creative energies operating from " above "; the moon and earth, representing the third Aspect, are the source of creative energies operating from " beneath ". Humanity represents the second Aspect and it is his task to forge the link which shall achieve the three-fold re-union.

76

# CREATIVE ENERGY: LUNAR, TERRENE AND SOLAR

Though the familiar terms moon, earth, sun; lunar, terrene, solar are convenient to use, it is of course the Life manifesting through these spheres which is the dominating factor. The sun is held to be the immediate vehicle of a mighty Being known as the Solar Logos. His three Aspects in manifestation within the solar system differ in their importance and dominance during rhythmic space-time periods. To the first Aspect is attributed the creative *Power* of the system; to the third Aspect the creative *Activity* concerned with planetary involution and the production of forms; and the second Aspect, with *Wisdom* as its attribute being dual in function, is said to operate with the third Aspect in the earlier cycles during the arc of involution, and with the first Aspect during the later cycles on the upward arc. It will be noted that, in the occult view, the sun—and the earth and moon also—represent vastly more than the totality of the physical properties they exhibit.

The moon, the relic of the one physical planet of Chain III, is claimed to have been the immediate parent of our earth. Its disintegration and the transfer of much of its educated material to the building of our world is the explanation of the very intimate relationship between this satellite and the earth, as also of the very similar qualities of the lunar and earthborn forces. Indeed lunar and terrene are now practically synonymous in this connection. The early Rounds of our Chain witnessed this transference from moon to earth together with the charging of the huge battery of the earth by the third Aspect of the One Life.

In Round I the initial building of the new earth-globe seems to have been the principal task. Solar energies of the first Aspect in the character of destroyer assisted in the disintegration of the moon planet, to be followed by the concentration of its material around its successor. Then, through the portals of the Web opened by the descending Life, the kingdoms of nature, led by human craftsmen, slowly developed their forms, and the electric charging of the earth began. The

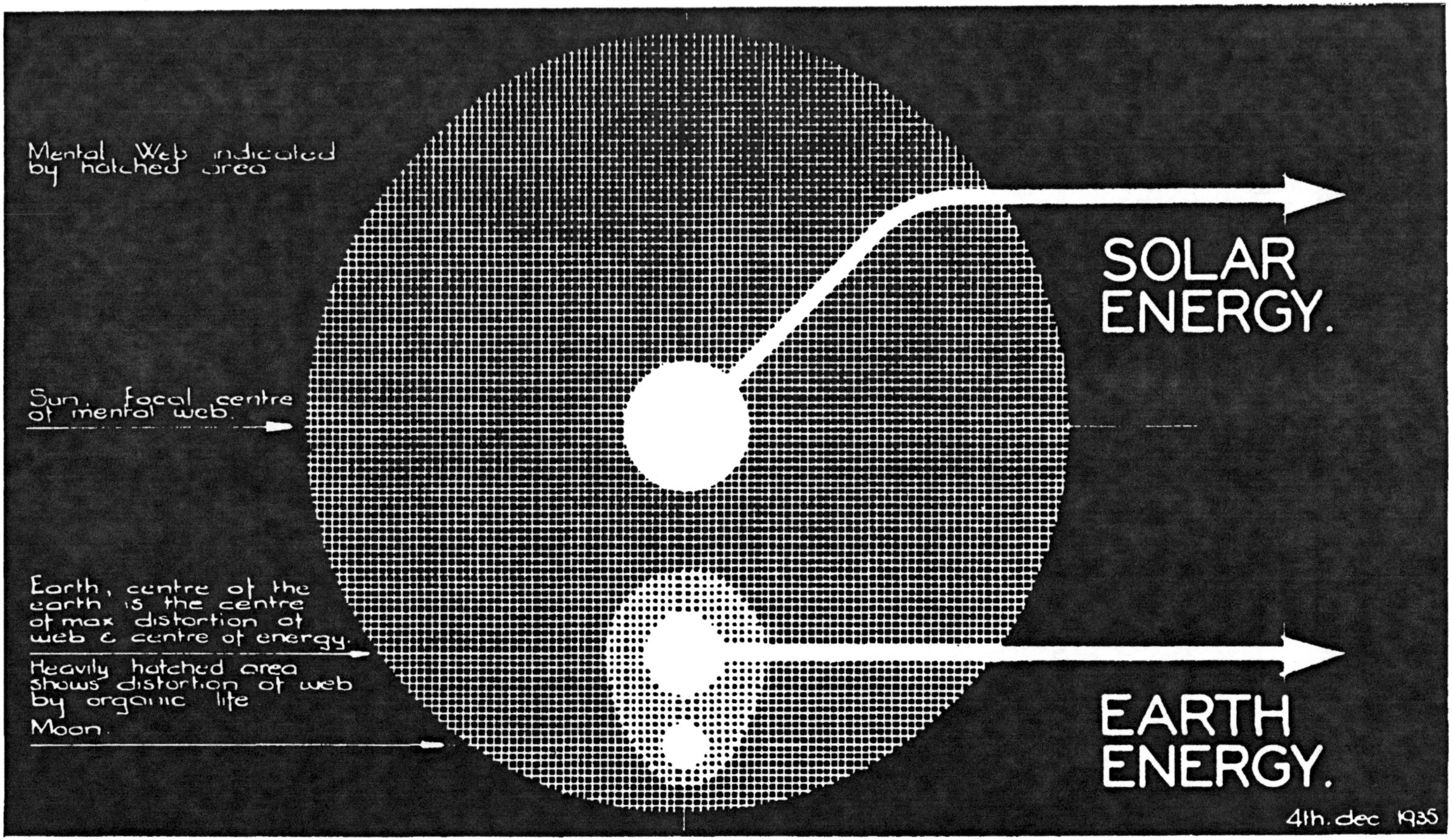

SOLAR
ENERGY.

EARTH
ENERGY.

4th. dec 1935

Mental Web indicated
by hatched area

Sun, focal centre
of mental web.

Earth, centre of the
earth is the centre
of max distortion of
web & centre of energy.

Heavily hatched area
shows distortion of web
by organic life
Moon.

mineral form was dominant in Round I and the plant form in Round II. Throughout this second Round the charging of the earth proceeded rapidly and continued during Round III until the earth became an enormously charged battery of energy. In Round IV, the present period, the development of the human form in physical solidity on our earth as we know it to-day (a projection of the archetypal human model in simple terms) has been achieved—and the earth battery now begins slowly to discharge.

In this diagram, the sun, the body of the Solar Logos, is shown as in the centre of the Web constituting the field of solar manifestation. For simplicity, our planet the earth alone is included together with its satellite. The energy stored within the mass of the earth has been collected during the first three Rounds, mostly during Round II via the forms of the then plant kingdom. During the early part of Round IV it has been held and stabilised in the mineral kingdom and now begins very slowly to be released. In the Vth, VIth and VIIth Rounds the release accelerates.

Of the forces distributed by the sun at the present time directly to the present-day evolutionary forms of the kingdoms of nature, the less potent are shared by all in terms of warmth, pranic currents and chemical action. The innermost, the finer and more intense, are modified (and to some extent intercepted) by certain orders of devas.* Humanity alone can respond to these, and only as the higher mind, the spiritual principle, awakens.

The following diagram, No. 25, is an attempt to indicate the vast cyclic processes whereby this task is accomplished, coupled as it necessarily is with the expansion, or rather release, of divine powers at present latent in man.

The immense fertility of the earth to-day is due largely to the gradual release of the energies stored within itself. The forms used now by mineral, plant and animal life all derive a sturdy vitality from the earth. From the sun also the forms

* Non-human agents of nature.

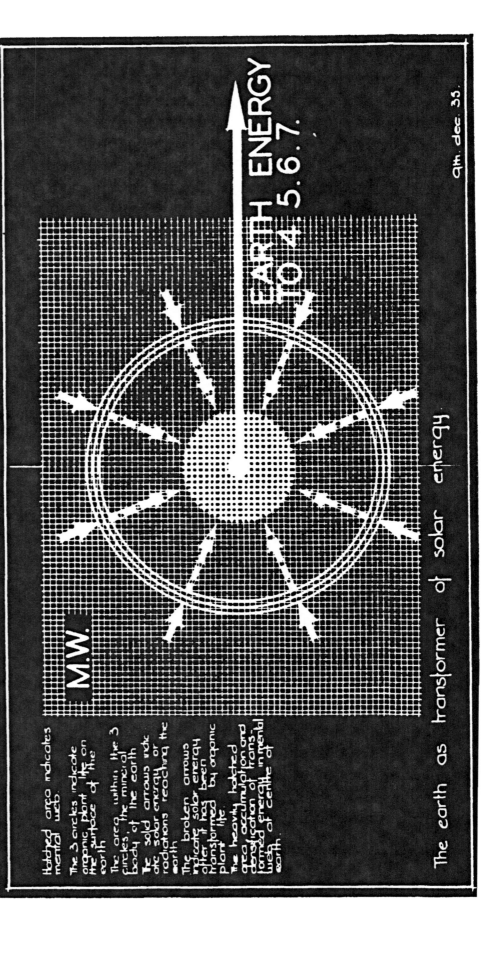

EARTH ENERGY 1. 2. 3. 4. 5. 6. 7.

M.W.

Hatched area indicates mental web.

The 3 circles indicate organic plant life on the surface of the earth.

The area within the 3 circles, the mineral body of the earth

The solid arrows indicate solar energy or radiations reaching the earth

The broken arrows indicate solar energy after it has been transformed by organic plant life.

The heavily hatched area accumulation and densification of transformed energy in mental web. of centre of earth.

The earth as transformer of solar energy.

CREATIVE ENERGY : LUNAR, TERRENE AND SOLAR

of the plant, animal and human kingdoms obtain a fiery sustenance in an increasing measure which each is able to use according to its growth and capacity.

Solar energy is here diagrammatically shown as being conducted through to the earth during the first three Rounds. The solid arrows touching the periphery of the circles represent solar energy reaching the earth. Through the early involutionary forms of the kingdoms of nature, mineral, plant and animal, on the mental, emotional and etheric planes respectively, the energy was transformed and accumulated in the earth. Therein it became locked up, coiled up is an expression used, as in a charged battery.

Lunar and terrene forces together nourish and support the personal bodies of man and are indispensable to their welfare. Indeed, just as in the plant kingdom roots are extended downwards first to secure a firm hold on the earth and water of bodily form before the upward thrust into the realm of sun and air is undertaken, so with man. The forces which strengthen and secure the grip of consciousness upon the personal life are the influences to which he first responds. This response, the result of a so-called temptation (as a familiar theological allegory has it) being achieved, human individualisation is won and established.

The successful shaping of formal bodies is attained under the shadow of the Lords of the Moon, the Barhishads, who were the hierarchical tutors of humanity in the control of physical forms, and of the Asura Hierarchy, whose tremendously difficult task of persuading our young hierarchy to enter the material " coats of skin " has earned for them the allegorical title of Satan.

The creative forces derived from the moon and the earth are by their nature unconscious within humanity, they are accepted and used primarily by the life of the elemental kingdoms functioning within human and animal bodies, and are automatic, vegetative and magnetic. Their influence in man's animal nature is displayed in the instincts of self-preservation,

81                                              F

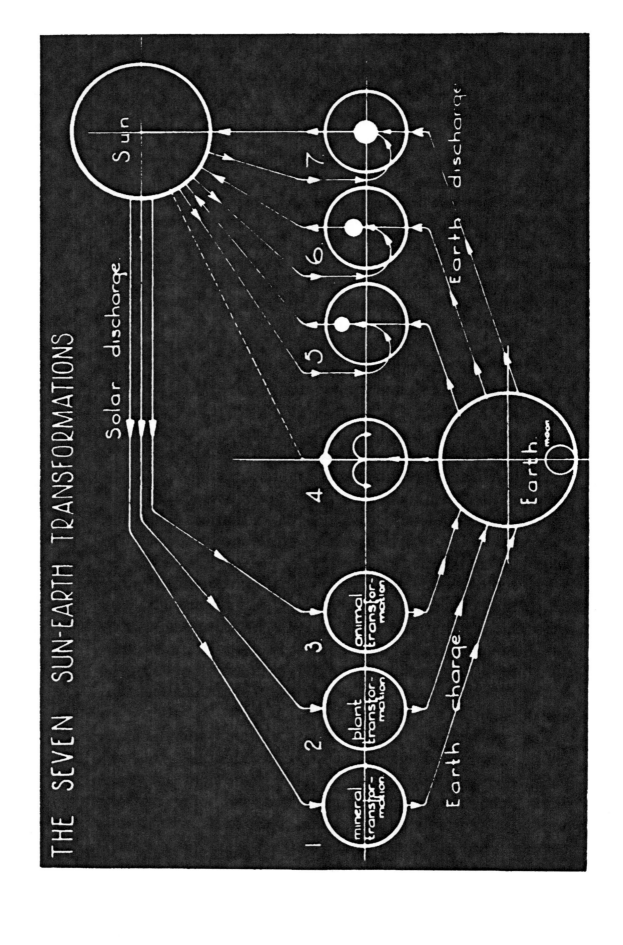

THE SEVEN SUN-EARTH TRANSFORMATIONS

possessiveness, jealousy and greed, all accentuated in the early animal forms used by our hierarchy in Round III and legitimately inherited by the animal kingdom at large.

The numbers 1 to 7 indicate the successive Rounds of our Chain, as in diagram No. 12. They also serve on a much smaller scale to indicate the seven Root-Races of our present world-occupation. (In this minor correspondence the circles 1 to 3 will represent in racial terms a rapid recapitulation of the Rounds and the circles 5 to 7 will represent brief racial rehearsals of the work of the future Rounds.)

The earth is shown as being charged by the sun during the long involutionary period and as discharging during the last three Rounds. In Round 4 a state of comparative stability obtains, for on the earth during this Round the turning point of the vast cycle is reached and passed.

The human form becomes dominant on Round 4 and its arrival is represented in the diagram by the white spot on the top of the middle circle. The arrows within this circle point downwards to mark the strong pressure of the terrene creative forces during this middle cycle. Nevertheless the solar influence begins to be potent and is represented by the dotted line traced directly from the sun to the human kingdom. In the cycles 5, 6 and 7 (slightly in the Root-Races, powerfully in Rounds) the solar influence in an accelerating degree leads to consummation in the human hierarchy in the 7th Round.

Through the human personal bodies the earth currents circulate by way of the sympathetic nervous system and the basic chakram of the spine connected with the sexual life. Rising normally as far as the heart they contribute to bodily strength and virility, to a good healthy tone and ample vigour of body. Their play can be stimulated by certain practices which may lead to feelings of intense physical well-being and exaltation. Some risk however lies in this direction notwithstanding the physical power obtained, because of the strong reaction of the sensory and instinctual emotions amounting to glamour. The terrene forces make for the health and vigour of the purely animal nature and an excess of them tends to stimulate the automatism of the elemental tendencies to the detriment of the truly human.

The position in which humanity finds itself to-day is somewhat critical in that the two opposite forces, terrene and solar, both of stimulating vitality and power in the human body, are nearly balanced. It is, too, increasingly within the range of human volition to decide as to what proportion of each shall be used. The lunar and terrene forces however have a tremendous momentum owing to their pressing dominance in the past on the involutionary arc, and this tends to out-weigh and obstruct the subtler influences of the solar light.

The power currents derived from the moon and earth as described are of such an easy flowing, accustomed, every-day character that they are utilised in the course of ordinary personal living too naturally and automatically to arouse any special interest or attention—except perhaps in the few who are philosophically inclined. But they can, unfortunately, be augmented and increased by adopting certain specific exercises. Some knowledge of such practices, dignified sometimes by the name magic, carries over from far-distant Atlantean times, and fragments of such information are a commercialised product that may be purchased even to-day —as witness many an advertisement in our periodicals offering the secrets of " power " for sale. The mark that brands them and informs the inquirer invariably and unmistakably of their nature is an association with money-making success and sexuality. A trace of these, early or late in its disclosure and however disguised, is sufficient evidence to condemn them as unworthy. The practices belong to the lunar cults of earlier Races, their value is outgrown, and the experiences engendered are retrogressive.

A significant feature introduced into the Mystery ceremonies by the hierarchical tutors of humanity, when the solar influences dawned in consciousness, was the symbolic marriage of solar and terrene energies. The original actors in such a rite were, in the ritual of the true Mysteries, officials of the highest rank, the lofty nature of the divine fires invoked being thus emphasised. Therefrom one may trace the idea of the indissolubility of the marriage tie—a veritable truth at the spiritual levels to which it referred but of little application in purely physical terms. Degeneration into phallic depths has marked many of those rites which, originally, were of a magnificent and lofty splendour. Even to-day a school of psychology, and one of the most widely popular, traces the creative fire in man to one source only, namely to the terrene —hence the prominence and overshadowing importance of sex in its conclusions and teaching; a half-truth. Fortunately, other schools, of increasing repute, recognise the higher faculties of man, the will and insight, as pertaining to and expressive of the Self, and their definitions of the Self are very close to a recognition of its spiritual nature and origin.

The work of the first three Rounds being completed and the fourth Round being half-way through, it follows that in the middle of our present world-occupation the turning point of the whole vast cycle of our Scheme was reached and passed and the upward arc begun. Individual consciousness having been established firmly in a body of dense material in the fourth Race on this earth, release from the bonds of matter is begun in our present fifth Race cycle, and the lost word of spiritual consciousness may again be heard.

A dramatic event of the first importance accompanied the turning point of the cycle, according to the occult tradition, for at this time there came the Lords of the Flame from the Venusian Planetary Scheme to take over the Inner Government of our world and to become the directive force in the evolution of our planetary life. The spark of mind was stimulated into activity and awakened in man, the *higher* mind being the first of his truly spiritual principles to respond. Their advent is probably the deeply hidden origin of the Chrestos and Solar Myths telling of the descent of a Saviour, an Avatar, a God.

By this coming the action of the solar energies in the human race was profoundly stimulated, for mind was and is the primary vehicle of the solar forces.

In relation to the physical body, the crown of the head is the power centre in man where solar energies are focused and whence they are directed and distributed. Fortunately for us the high potencies of solar fire can be consciously invoked and used only by a mind which has been in considerable measure disciplined and clarified. Humanity is not yet widely self-conscious concerning these high contacts, though their influence is abundantly registered in the very numerous charitable and altruistic movements found in all civilised countries at the present time. The free play of solar forces waits always on some measure of personal sacrifice.

The inner solar forces drawn directly from the sun are thus beginning to function in humanity. Entering through the head they also reach the heart and there, combining with the terrene stream, endow humanity with the promise of awakening powers which may indeed be illimitable in their scope. In the heart of man is the real at-one-ment made, by the linking of the Life forces of the first and third Aspects, for man, in his collective capacity as the fourth Creative Hierarchy, is the living Bridge in our vast Solar Scheme. Of interesting significance here is the story told in the old mystery drama of the birth of the Christ-Child in a stable or cave, for the cave of the mystery teaching corresponds to the home of the animal, the heart of man. Highest and lowest meet in the heart.

Two sources of creative power are thus within man's conscious reach to-day, for he stands midway, so to speak, between the solar " fire " and the terrene " water ", olden names for the two cosmic forces. Both are necessary and vital to humanity, for unless both are accepted, used and balanced, the true human stature cannot be attained. To distinguish clearly between solar and terrene sources of power is difficult until some lucid and impersonal thinking and feeling have been practised, coupled with a certain detached analysis of oneself. The only real test available for a student's use is the validity of his own experience honestly interpreted. Distinctions on broad lines are easy to classify and the following tables indicate some of these as examples:

Prompted from lunar and terrene creative sources:

> Thinking of an automatic, repetitive character; mechanical reverie, idle day-dreaming, etc.
> Instincts of self-protection, self-interest, acquisitiveness, tending to fear and cowardice.
> Hunger and thirst; sexual desire.
> Dictates of the conventional conscience. The passive psychic medium.
> Sympathetic nervous system. Learning by rote. Copying.
> In religious discipline, negative precepts such as the Jewish ten commandments. Penances.

Prompted (inspired) from solar creative sources:

> Self-initiated thought.
> Intuitive love, loyalty, probity, courage, truthfulness, etc.
> Creative art in music, poetry, dancing, etc. Invention.
> Controlled psychism of the Seer.
> Cerebro-spinal nervous system. Breathing (partially).
> In religious discipline, the golden rule. Meditation.

The creative power from the sun is, comparatively, but slight at present though ultimately to be as readily and naturally accepted as that from "beneath". To strengthen the solar flow, indeed to recognise it at all for what it is, demands self-directed and voluntary effort. Such effort has its own magic and its own specialised methods.

In a search for guidance the student will find a large variety of ancient myths and cults to interest him, mystery teachings and ceremonies picturing the relation of sun to moon and man's relation to both, of the sacrifice of solar energies on the cross of matter, of death and resurrection (or re-birth), dramatised usually by the help of a liberal cast of deities who personify god-like and human attributes. Among them may be traced many a hint and much instruction concerning a practice which appears again and again in later periods and in all faiths. This is the withdrawal of the individual consciousness from the dominance of sensation and emotion and other earth-born stimuli—and the deliberate cultivation of contact with an interior light, an inner vision, the dis-covery of a spiritual centre, of the God within. Instruction in this has accompanied the turn of the cycle of manifestation from the downward to the upward arc.

The science of the union of individual consciousness and the solar Life is called to-day, both in east and west, the science of yoga. It is in effect the science of the union of the terrene forces with the solar, the re-union of the third and first Aspects of the one Life through man—for man bears within himself the sacred fire of the second Aspect which alone can link the twain. Thus, through man, solar energy can dominate and control the instinctual life drawn from lunar and terrene sources. By self-directed and voluntary effort contact may be established with the solar centre in the head, the seat (in physical terms) of the higher consciousness, the higher self. It is in and from this centre, strictly speaking in the higher mind, that the higher creative powers of the solar Life are focused, reflected and expressed through our present human consciousness.

Efforts on these lines have been confined in the past to the few who were capable of the consistent struggle and selflessness demanded. To-day, since the turn of the cycles is well past its half-way mark, many may contact and distribute the inner light—if they will. The veils of bodily form are beginning to wear thin and the awakening into activity of long dormant faculties under the influence of the finer grades of the solar light begins. Privation has done its work, compelling concentration, and humanity in many directions is claiming true self-awareness as its birthright. Understanding discrimination is the first step in yoga—awakened spirituality follows close upon its heels.

The theme of all mystery ceremonies has been and is the dis-covery and awakening of that centre of spiritual life, the focus of divinity, in every human being. Though man shares the one and universal Life pervading all that is manifest and actually is immersed in it, the birth and realisation in human consciousness of the immanence of the solar light is always the discovery as of a light within—the centre is a dis-covered sanctuary of light within one's very being. The sacrifice by the terrene personality of its long-accustomed first place in the interest and attention of consciousness is the prelude to a release of the solar creative forces, and these, in the course of the cycle, may make of truly self-conscious man a Prometheus Unbound.

> " There is an inmost centre in us all
>     Where truth abides in fulness; . . . and to know
>   Rather consists in opening out a way
>     Whence the imprisoned splendour may escape
> Than in effecting entry for a light
>     Supposed to be without."
>
> *Paracelsus*, BROWNING

The field of manifestation we have attempted to envisage presents itself as a stupendous unfoldment of power on a pattern at once simple and immensely complex. Simple inasmuch as it proceeds on the lines of a constantly repeated design and hence can be elucidated with the key of correspondences; yet complex to an infinite degree by reason of the interweaving and overlapping of its patterns as consciousness, born from Life amid the friction of opposing forms, strives to attain the secret of being. From our study there may emerge perhaps a fuller understanding of the lofty and pioneer role played by man on a stage of finely tuned sub-stance prepared and furnished with all the material properties needed for Life's manifestation and experience.

# APPENDIX

## OUR SOLAR SCHEME

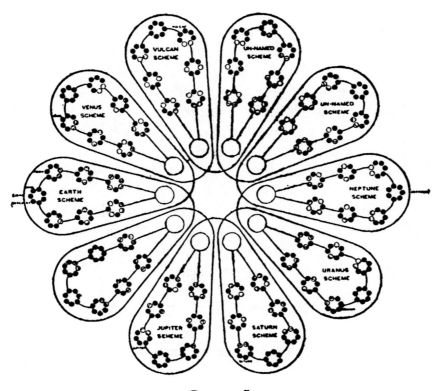

Chart I

The Ten Schemes of the Solar System are displayed in the above Chart diagrammatically. Each Scheme is shown separately with its seven Chains. The Ten Schemes are all in manifestation together, each proceeding on its own lines. The seven Chains within each Scheme are actually successive, only one Chain of globes being in existence at one time. The globes of these chains are also displayed separately simply for the sake of clarity; strictly they can be regarded as " separate " only in the fourth Chain of each series.

Of the ten Schemes, seven only are represented by physical globes, hence three are unnamed. The One Solar Life is functioning in all, but is at different stages of growth and development in the different Schemes, and hence the Schemes differ in age or stage of development. The Chain of globes in each Scheme that is in manifestation now is known by the name of its densest planet. These are the Seven Sacred Planets of occult literature, of which our earth is one.

Omitting the Vulcan and Neptunian Schemes, about which little information is given, the eldest and most advanced appears to be that of Venus, the second is the Terrene, our own, and Jupiter comes next.

Though the Life streams of the Schemes are not inter-connected directly these last-named three are related somewhat intimately. In the interests of the cosmic economy of the mighty Solar System, Venus has vitally assisted and is assisting our Terrene evolution. We may infer that similar help will be extended by us to the Jupiterian in due course.

With regard to the differing and special task of each Scheme very little is intimated. We might possibly and reasonably surmise the principle and plane, or group of both, with which each is particularly concerned, but it would be largely speculative and merely academic. So we may turn to the fuller information relating to our own Scheme and present Chain.

## OUR TERRENE SCHEME

In each Planetary Scheme there are seven successive incarnations or circuits of the great Life Waves from the Solar Logos.

On each Chain, from the first onwards, all the stages of consciousness known as the kingdoms of nature, from the elemental to the human, are present. The broad rule appears to be that, for the span of a Chain, a given impulse of the Logoic consciousness functions through the forms of one kingdom only.

Success with these forms means that in the next succeeding Chain that same impulse of consciousness qualifies to enter the forms of the next higher kingdom. It should be always remembered that there are no hard and fast dividing lines and hence considerable over-lapping arises, but the general rule is that the Life Wave of the Logos overshadows the forms of one kingdom of nature and then passes on in the next chain to overshadow the next and more evolved kingdom, e.g., the Life Wave that used the mineral forms in a First Chain will enter and use plant forms in a Second Chain period.

Owing to varying experiences the step from one kingdom to the next may occur at any period during a Chain's progress. This tendency becomes especially pronounced when the middle period of a Chain is approached. Such overlapping becomes confusing unless the flexibility of the evolving life is held in mind together with the underlying law.

The field of action differs for each Chain, but in each four planes only are touched.

Chain I. Called *Brahmah's Body of Darkness*. Field of Action: Atma, Buddhi, H. Manas and L. Manas. Lower Mental was the densest and the crux.

Chain II. The boundaries are *life* planes and the Chain is known as *Brahmah's Body of Light*. Field of Action: Buddhi, H. Manas, L. Manas, Astral.

Chain III. Bounded by the higher sections of form planes and called *Brahmah's Body of Twilight*. Field of Action: H. Manas, L. Manas, Astral, H. Physical.

Chain IV. Of the seven Chains comprising our Terrene Scheme, it is the fourth on which we find ourselves to-day. The present Chain sees the turning point of the Scheme as a whole and is known as *Brahmah's Body of Dawn*. Field of Action: L. Manas, Astral, H. Physical and Dense Physical.

The student should note that the field of experience open to any one kingdom on a Chain is not identical with that of its successor on the next. The field differs and hence the experiences are dissimilar. The consciousness functioning through the plant kingdom of our second Chain, for instance, would have very different experiences from the plant consciousness of the third Chain, for the latter would have a new and denser plane as its basic material. The life within each of the kingdoms of our planet to-day, therefore, has followed its own unique course.

One of the seven paths open to the successful humanity of any Chain is that of assisting the evolving life of the following Chain. Indeed, if this path be chosen it seems that the assistance is rendered to at least the three following Chains of the Scheme. The humanity of Chain I of the Terrene system for instance, known as the 5th Creative Hierarchy (*vide infra*), is still in touch with our

Scheme. The Asuras, as they are designated owing to the office they at present fill, have influenced our humanity through the mental, particularly the lower mental, principle. The 6th Hierarchy, the Agnishvattas of the 2nd Chain, influences us through the emotions and intuitions, the Barhishads of the 3rd Chain assist and have always assisted us in the building of bodies.

The interest and the application of all this to us lie in its indication of our responsibilities to the younger kingdoms of the mineral, plant and animal. For, obviously, applying the Chain-Kingdom rule, our own relation to the animal kingdom is similar to that of the Barhishads to us. Our relation to the plant life is that of the Agnishvattas to us, and to the mineral that of the Asuras to us. Our present and ordinary attitudes to those lower kingdoms is evidence of the major law of correspondence stated above. Our attitude to the mineral life for instance is quite naturally and unaffectedly one of cold detached mentality. The emotional nature is seldom stirred and, except in the case of jewels perhaps, rarely stimulated. To the flowering plants, and vegetation generally, our relation is just as naturally emotional. Concerning the animals, H.P.B.'s statements regarding the bodily legacy humanity has left to them (*S.D. Vol. II*) are illuminating indeed. Thus in the study of the Chains and the inter-relation of the Hierarchies is to be found the key to the understanding of our intimate responsibilities to the evolving life of the kingdoms below us.

# THE SEVEN CHAINS OF THE EARTH SCHEME

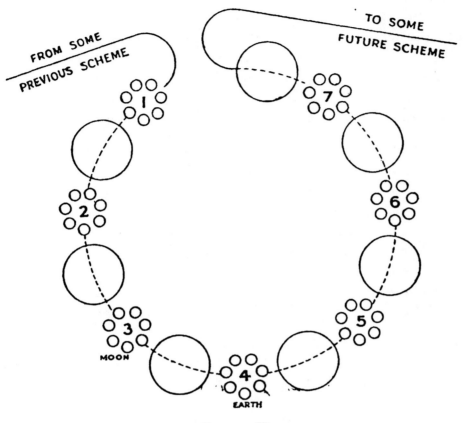

CHART II

Assisted by Chart II our study of the Terrene Scheme can be continued to better advantage. The seven successive Chains of globes, expressing the form side of manifestation, are clearly displayed, and the periods of pralaya (the life side) are indicated by the spheres between the Chains.

From a previous Scheme of an earlier System the life commences on Chain I, and all the Kingdoms are therein represented.

The seven kingdoms are the 1st, 2nd, and 3rd Elemental Kingdoms, Mineral, Plant, Animal and Human. These are all engaged in the work of Chain I. Seven circuits (Rounds) of the globes in a Chain are made, under the general superintendence and within the mighty being of the Root-Manu. A Chain of globes may indeed be regarded as the Root-Manu's bodily form, an incarnation as it were.

95

At the conclusion of the work of a Chain the Life is gathered into the aura of the Seed-Manu for a vast cosmic sleep of assimilation and recuperation. Therein, during the interchain pralaya, the consciousness of the kingdoms is smoothed out, disentangled and adjusted, and made ready to engage in the work of the next Chain of globes. The Seed Manu's aura is sometimes represented in regular bands of colour to suggest the ordered harmony resulting from the pralaya or rest period.

The following tables epitomise certain information given:

THE OCCULT GOVERNMENT OF THE TERRENE SCHEME:

1. The Logos of the Solar System, the Life of the 10 Schemes.
2. The Ruler of the Earth Scheme. (One of the Spirits before the Throne.)
3. The Root and Seed Manus of a Chain.
4. The Root and Seed Manus of a single Round.
5. The Lord of the World.
6. The Buddhas.
7. The Manu (form) and the Bodhisattva (life) of a Root-Race.

THE HIERARCHIES AND THEIR CHAINS:

Chain I: The Fifth Creative Hierarchy: 7 Globes—Atma to Lower Mental.

„ II: The Sixth Creative Hierarchy: 7 Globes—Buddhi to Astral.

„ III: The Seventh Creative Hierarchy: 7 Globes—H. Mental to H. Physical.

„ IV: The Fourth Creative Hierarchy: (Our Humanity) 7 Globes—L. Mental to Dense Physical.

THE GOAL SET FOR HUMANITY OF EACH CHAIN:

Chain I: The First Initiation. (4th Hierarchy then in Mineral Kingdom.)

„ II: The Third Initiation. (4th Hierarchy then in Vegetable Kingdom.)

„ III: The Fourth Initiation. (4th Hierarchy then in Animal Kingdom.)

„ IV: The Fifth Initiation. (4th Hierarchy in Human Kingdom.)

# APPENDIX

The attainment of the goal set qualifies for entrance on one of the seven paths of service:

The Seven Choices before the Perfect Man:

1. Remains with Humanity as an official of the Hierarchy. (Form.)
2. Remains with Humanity as a " Nirmanakaya ". (Life.)
3. Joins the Devas or Angelic Hosts.
4. Joins the " Staff Corps of the Logos ".
5. Prepares the work of the next Chain.
6 & 7. Enters Nirvana.

Though the Chains are successive, each representing practically a reincarnation of the last, no sudden ending or beginning must be assumed. On the last Round of a Chain, as the concentrated effort of the Root-Manu passes from Globe A onwards, the earlier globes dissolve (instead of retiring merely into obscuration as on previous Rounds) and their principles are carried over to the construction of corresponding globes of the succeeding Chain. Hence the work of the new Chain is begun long before that of the last is concluded. Even now, for instance, though we are only half-way through the 4th Chain, the preliminary work of the 5th is already in hand.

After the period of pralaya the life of the kingdoms passes on from the Seed-Manu to the Root-Manu in a regular sequence and a general rule may again be noted. The earlier Rounds of a Chain furnish the field most suited for the younger and less advanced grades of consciousness of all the kingdoms and the later Rounds for the more advanced and older. Hence much of the more evolved life taken over by the Seed-Manu towards the close of a Chain is not passed on to incarnation on the succeeding Chain till a late period in that Chain. An environment corresponding in a measure to that experienced in the last Chain is usually first secured. This means that the most advanced individuals and units of life do not enter a succeeding Chain till its middle period or even later.

Indeed we may gather, for instance, that some of the most evolved of the third Chain are only now coming in—on the fourth globe of the fourth Round of this.

G

The Chain-Kingdom rule referred to earlier (one kingdom for the term of one Chain) should be understood as meaning in nearly all cases 7 Rounds, for these 7 Rounds may frequently be spread over two Chains for the reasons set out in the last paragraph.

## DEVA AND HUMAN:

In the middle period of the mineral kingdom it seems that Life, having then arrived at its deepest immersion in form, divides into two streams. One follows on through the jewels and then, through grasses and cereals, on to insects, birds and all winged creatures. Leaving the dense physical plane at this last stage the next and later steps are taken among the deva hosts. The other stream of Life, following through the metals and on through mosses, shrubs, trees, etc., reaches the mammalia in the animal kingdom and thence from the seven types of domesticated animals at length the human. This outline is given to indicate that a successful Hierarchy includes highly developed beings of both the human and devic (angelic) type.

A very interesting and instructive fact may be inferred from the occult teaching concerning the relations of the Deva and Human evolutions. Though parallel streams of life their relative importance changes. First the Deva, then the Human, in any cycle seems to be the practice. The dominant life of Chains I, II and III was that of the Devas and Nature Spirits. In comparison the Human throughout appears to have been subordinate, though tending strongly towards a balance as the Scheme proceeded. In the 4th Chain this relation becomes gradually reversed and Man must fill the role of pioneer and leader. The half-way point of balance is passed and humanity is slowly assuming control—very little conscious at present, however, of his powers. The present experiments in harnessing nature, so evident in the machinery of our current civilisation, are a slight earnest of the future.

The Coming of the Kumaras, members of the humanity of the Venus Scheme, to take over the charge of the Earth inaugurated this reversal. We are witnessing the change taking place at this very period of the 4th Round's course. Its tremendous import for our humanity cannot be over-estimated and the recognition and understanding of our task should enlist the attention of every student of occultism.

# APPENDIX

## THE SEVEN GLOBES OF THE EARTH CHAIN

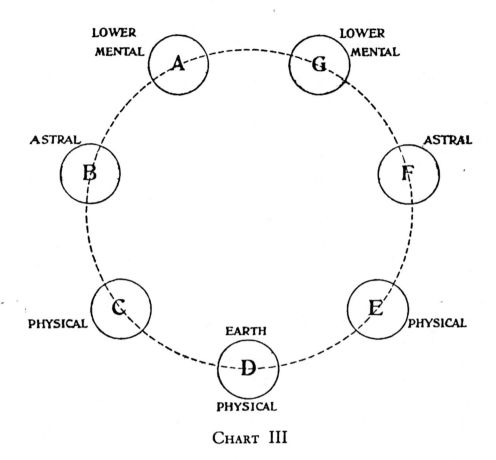

CHART III

The life of the kingdoms is passed on to the Earth Chain of globes from the aura of the interchain Seed-Manu. The Root-Manu in charge of the Chain accepts the younger life first and the first Round, commencing on globe A, is begun. The seven globes appear each to be separate and distinct on this the 4th Chain and the life stream makes the Round from globe A to G and then repeats the circuit in the second and subsequent Rounds.

Three Rounds of the globes have been made and the fourth is in progress now, the life being concentrated on globe D. Indeed it is the prodigious concentration of the Root-Manu on the globes in turn that occasions the circuit. The globes from which the life has passed on remain in slight activity only—in obscuration it is called—till the life stream reaches them again in the next Round.

A correspondence to much of this is found in our own personality. The sleep of the physical body at night denotes the transference of activity to the next subtler vehicle. The physical body is in obscuration till the morning. Similarly for brief periods during the day, if the mind be exercised in thought alone, the physical body is out of focus, obscured. Concentration decides the instrument that shall be active.

A study of the Earth Chain is a study in essence of the whole Scheme. Just as in embryology one may trace the evolution of the physical form through all the earlier stages of development from the simple cell, so in the first three Rounds of our Chain the work of the first three Chains is recapitulated. On these Rounds certain work is done rapidly that took untold ages of effort on the earlier Chains. The Scheme works onwards to the climax of its involution in the fourth Round of its fourth Chain.

In the fourth Round our humanity takes a share in the pioneer task of the building of the new forms. In this respect the Round differs from all the preceding, and the narrative outlined in the S.D., Vol. II, Part III, is of profound interest to-day.

The Rounds are the big and important divisions of a Chain's manifestation.

During the fourth Round balance and adjustment are achieved and three final Rounds comprise the synthetic culminating work of the Chain. The urge of the life on the first three Rounds is towards the outermost of vehicles and principles—the physical; the urge on the three last is to return towards the innermost. The middle, the present, Round is involved in the keen struggle attending the use and mastery of the densest body touched in the whole Chain.

The fifth Round, the first of the synthetic three, is concerned with the Mental principle and its perfection. This entails the complete development and use of the causal body (the spiritual, the "celestial" body) as an instrument of self-consciousness and the unfolding of the divine faculty of omnipresence. The fifth Round too, it is said, witnesses the "day of judgment" a period of sorting out and adjustment in which those Egos offering no promise of attaining the goal of the Chain are withdrawn from further participation in its work. In the aura of the Seed-Manu they are said to await the development of the next Chain to a suitable point before they can proceed further. The sixth Round is concerned with the Intuitional principle, and its perfection leads to omniscience. The seventh Round similarly with the Will, the perfection of which principle means omnipotence within the limits of our Scheme. Such an attainment as this is so vast as to be incomprehensible at present, yet contained in the simple precept " Be ye therefore perfect even as your Father . . ." (Matt. V, 48) and in the promise of another ancient scripture " the soul of man is immortal and its future growth and splendour have no limits ".

The following table sets out in brief the inter-relations mentioned :

| | |
|---|---|
| 7 Sub-Races - - - - - | 1 Root-Race |
| 7 Root-Races - - - - - | 1 World-Period |
| 7 World-Periods - - - | 1 Round |
| 7 Rounds - - - - - - | 1 Chain |
| 7 Chains - - - - - - | 1 Scheme |

---

| | |
|---|---|
| 7 & 3 Schemes - - - - | The Solar System |

The Sub-races are like children in a family—they are successive in birth and then are contemporary; for instance, the five sub-races of the fifth Root-Race are all numerically represented to-day in the world.

The Root-Races similarly. The third (Black), fourth (Yellow), and fifth (White) are the humanity of to-day, in incarnation.

The Globes again similarly, though here the dominance of one is more pronounced.

The immediate application of all this to our own times is that just as the first three Races of our earth were recapitulatory of the earlier Rounds, so the last three Races are anticipatory of the work to be accomplished on the fifth, sixth and seventh Rounds. That which will be the common achievement of average humanity in these later Rounds is just possible of achievement by *individuals* of our humanity to-day. The division of the sexes that occurred in the third Race corresponded to a similar process in the third

Round, and the fifth Round will see the complementary reunion in the divine hermaphrodite. Our fifth Race foreshadows this in the case only of the loftiest of our humanity.

We are in the fifth Root-Race (and the fifth sub-race of that) and hence particularly is the principle of Mind dominant—with its limitation and illumination. The lower mind in the previous Race, in association with the emotional nature (form and life), was developed to a marvellous degree of automatic responsiveness to sensation. Everything sensed is recorded indelibly in the lower mind though we may not realise it in waking consciousness. This amazing aptitude of the lower mind is the triumphant culmination of the work of the earlier Rounds in general and of our own first four Races in particular. The methods employed may be traced by the student intent on pursuing this study in greater detail, assisted by the symbolism of the world religions as set out in the *S.D.* The mystery of the subconsciousness—(the subject of so much psychological research to-day)—and its faculty of passive retentiveness are both revealed in such a study.

The fifth Round task is the realisation by humanity of the powers of the higher mind in conjunction with the lower—their union in short. That which applies to average humanity in terms of Rounds may be anticipated by individuals in terms of Races here and now.

The Mind is the instrument of understanding, and the occult teaching implies that it must be prepared for its mission of serving as the channel of wisdom before that sixth Round when Wisdom will be arrayed in all her glory.

The advent of the sixth sub-race of this the fifth Root-Race and the fact that from it the great sixth Root-Race will be born makes the study of the Rounds of immediate application. Evidence of the spirit of service and co-operation is not wanting and, though we live in early times comparatively, the ancient wisdom points the way of progress unerringly for those who will see.

E. L. G.

# REFERENCES

*The Secret Doctrine*, Vols. I, II, III   -   H. P. BLAVATSKY
        (Third Edition)

*A Study in Consciousness*  -    -    -   ANNIE BESANT
*First Principles of Theosophy*    -    -   C. JINARAJADASA
*The Inner Life* -    -    -    -    -   C. W. LEADBEATER
*Growth of the Soul*   -    -    -    -   A. P. SINNETT

The Library, The Theosophical Society, 50 Gloucester Place, London, W.1.

Theosophical Publishing House, 68 Great Russell Street, London, W.C.1.

Printed in the United States
90091LV00006B/107-110/A